Archangels and Earthangels

Petra Schneider • Gerhard K. Pieroth

Archangels and Earthangels

An Inspiring Handbook on Spiritual Helpers
In the Metaphysical and Earthly Spheres

Translated by Christine M. Grimm

ARCANA
PUBLISHING

Archangels and Earthangels do not make the visit to a doctor, naturopath, or psychotherapist superfluous when there is suspicion of a serious health disorder.

The information in this book has been presented to the best of our knowledge and conscience. Despite this fact, the authors do not assume any liability whatsoever for damages of any type that may occur through the direct or indirect application of the LightBeings Master Essences or utilization of the statements in this book.

"LightBeings" and "Master Essences" are protected trademarks by Dr. Petra Schneider.

First English Edition 2000
© by Arcana Publishing
an imprint of Lotus Brands, Inc.
P.O. Box 325
Twin Lakes, WI 53181, USA
Published in cooperation
with Schneelöwe Verlagsberatung, Federal Republic of Germany
© 1999 reserved by the Windpferd Verlagsgesellschaft mbH, Aitrang
All rights reserved
Translated by Christine M. Grimm
Edited by Karen Crane
Cover design by Kuhn Graphik, Digitales Design, Zürich, Switzerland, by using a draft of Dominik Lommer, Munich and Petra Diefenbach, Mühltal, Germany

ISBN 0-910261-19-9
Library of Congress Catalog Number 00-131346

Printed in USA

Table of Contents

You who we love
You do not see us
You do not hear us.
You think we are far off in the distance
And yet we are so near.
We are messengers
Who bring closeness to those far away
Who bring light to those in the dark
Who bring the word to those who question.
We are not the light, we are not the message
We are the messengers.

From Wim Wender's film *Faraway, So Close!*

Introduction

We all know that angels perform miracles. People who believe in angels usually think that they are here to help humans do what we can't do for ourselves.

I have discovered that this is true: Angels are here to help us. Their actions are more obvious when they perform something incredible, like helping a person survive a terrible car accident or recover from a life-threatening disease. These occurrences are awesome and wonderful; they allow us a glimpse of the enormous power of angels.

Since I know that angels are here to help humans and that they have powers far beyond anything we can even imagine, I have often wondered: Is there more? Is it possible to access angelic power, wisdom, and love every day of my life, even for the most mundane activities? Can angels be like partners who I can turn to for inspiration in all matters? Do they offer me awareness beyond my own powers of perception?

I was happy to discover that the answer to all of these questions is "yes!" During the past several years, I have spent much time exploring exactly how this works and what it means for my daily life. I have consciously invited the angels into countless everyday situations, and the results have been amazing. Especially my growth in terms of spirituality and everyday life has been greatly accelerated. Accepting the angels as my partners has freed me from many emotional blocks, ineffective mental habits, and negative behavior patterns. Furthermore, I have released many burdens that I carried from the past. Now I am finally growing up instead of just getting older. I am aware of my increased maturity and finally feel more confident about facing situations in a way that supports my value system. This gives me a sense of pride. When viewed individually, the single instances of angelic help may seem insignificant; but when they are perceived as a sequence, a powerful picture emerges. I can see many moments in which I have chosen to avoid suffering and instead moved toward the actions that fulfill me. As a result, I have had more fun and more joy in life.

Being a partner with the angels gives me a subtle advantage in almost any everyday situation. Incredible miracles are wonderful, but I have benefited even more by learning to ask for guidance every time I am unsure or unhappy with my own actions. Through practice, I have become better at clearly receiving these messages from the angels. Then I can use this information to make different choices about my own reactions to situations.

For example, my husband recently took his son from a previous marriage away for the weekend while I stayed at home, looking after our jointly owned business. By the time my husband returned, I was drained and tired from working alone all weekend. He showed up in a bad mood, and I felt angry and cheated. My initial reaction was to think that he had the entire weekend off, while I had to work the whole time—he should be in a good mood at least! Because I consciously invite the angels to interact with me in these situations, they immediately filled my mind with different words. I felt them override my own thoughts and heard them say: "He is as worn out as you are. Like you, he needs to feel understood. Open your arms, hug him, and ask him what he's feeling. Will that deplete any of your own energy? Watch what happens if you are compassionate." In that same moment, I felt myself filled with fresh energy, love, and a deep silence. I hugged my husband and listened to him without complaining. Then I noticed how quickly he recovered, and how beautifully we connected in silence afterward. As soon as he felt revived, he noticed all the work that I had done over the weekend and acknowledged my efforts with much appreciation and praise. For me, this was a valuable lesson about what happens when I am able to shift out of a negative mood or bad habit. Best of all, I learned this lesson—thanks to the conscious guidance of the angels—without suffering through a quarrel that might have otherwise developed.

Angelic guidance has been most useful to me when I am faced with situations that trigger my most intense disempowering patterns. One of these many fears has been about not having enough money. I recently watched in agony as our bank balance would jump from surprising heights to unexpected depths. It seemed that the money disappeared exactly when bills were due. We were stuck in the rut of working hard all day long, sleeping only a few hours a night, and starting back up again early the next morning. Our physical energy levels were decreasing, and we were even more drained by the lack of improvement in the financial situation. One day, I hit rock bottom, convinced that I was a victim of an evil world. I shouted at the angels: "What else can I do? I have given everything!"

Their response was profound and practical: "If you don't nurture and take care of yourself, if you overextend yourself, isn't it natural that your bank account will reflect this? See the amount of money in the bank as a mirror of your own energy level, an indicator of your own depletion!" A light clicked on in my head. This had become a familiar pattern for me. Even though I had been consciously working on releasing it for years, I was still clinging to my old, stuck concepts of money and success. The angelic guidance, which comes in the form of vibrational sensations in addition to words, finally brought this pattern to the light and made me aware of the solution. At that moment, I promised to take better care of myself, to focus on achieving rejuvenation and fulfillment, and to maintain a healthy balance between work and play.

When I checked our account the next day, I found a large and unexpected payment from a customer we had given up on. This was certainly a clear lesson, which also had an obvious reward for learning it.

Now that I consciously invite them in, the angels have become a permanent part of my life. I know that they are by my side at all times. With infinite patience, they show me time and over again how I create my own obstacles. They also make me aware of the ways in which I ignore my intuition and compromise myself. I realize that they have always been there for me—they have even tried to communicate with me. But I couldn't or wouldn't hear them. In choosing a partnership with the angels, I allow this subtle voice to speak and give my ears permission to hear it. This is a very miraculous way to live.

In our explorations with the angels, my husband and I have received much information that has not previously appeared in a book. As spiritual aspirants, we would like to share what we have learned with others. As engineers, our passion has become writing about these topics while using our perceptive powers to investigate the information beyond the level of our own personal concerns.

We have gathered a large wealth of knowledge about the angels that is applicable to everyone. This rare information is offered at our workshops and in this book. At the core of our work is a unique way of viewing the world, based on our experiences with the personalities and essences of the nine archangels and seven earthangels. We are happy to share this knowledge and these experiences with you.

These types of miracles are possible every day, for each of us, including yourself. Angels are always at our side, encouraging and supporting us in the development of our spiritual and godlike natures. They help us unfold these aspects of our being in our day-to-day lives. We have found this to be the true definition of "maturity." Personally speaking, we like our mature selves much better than our immature selves. Inviting angels into your everyday life will lead you to living the life that you love. We encourage you to try this approach because we sincerely believe that you will also discover that the benefits are fantastic.

We are building a new homepage so that we can enter into a conversation with you, as well as share insights and the most current information. Its name is www.morethanmiracles.com. You can also visit our other homepage at www.lightbeings-essences.com for more information, sharing, and networking. It also includes our schedule for visits to places all over this beautiful world. You can check it to see where we will be to share information, hold meditation events and seminars, or simply be available for meetings with interested readers.

Steps to Perception

A Different View of the World

This book describes a philosophy of the world, a model. People who work with the powers of the angels have a different view of the world than those who consider everything incomprehensible to be nonsense. And precisely here is the difference between the rationalists and the esoteric/spiritual human being. In the eyes of a rationalist, the universe consists only of matter; for the latter, a subtle world exists in addition to the material world.

Once we recognize this fundamental difference in philosophy between the two groups, then there is no longer any reason to fight or try to convince others. There is no evidence (at least not yet) of the subtle, spiritual realm. It is a different concept of the world. We can compare this to Galileo developing a different concept of the world with the image of the earth orbiting around the sun. The Church's belief was that the sun circled around the stationary disk of the earth. The model of the spiritual world, the subtle energies, and the angels must also withstand a reality check. It may be easy to develop many imaginative theories, yet they must also function in terms of earthly reality.

People—including myself—who are in contact with angels and make use of their powers, see the effects of this. Old forms of behavior are discontinued more quickly than they would normally be and requests are fulfilled. Therapists notice that more happens during their sessions, and impossible things or miracles occur. These powers have been effective for me, as well as for many other people.

This naturally isn't proof of anything. But these are experiences. And in order to have these experiences, we must be willing to open up and undergo them. Which is why I often recommend the following: Go ahead and try it out! What do you have to lose? Ask the angels to do something for you such as resolving a deadlocked situation, giving you the answer to a question, or making it possible for you to encounter a certain person. Be willing to have this experience. But be careful—even when what we wished for occurs or something happens, the rational mind or the well-worn old concept of the world will not accept this as the work of the angels. There is a great deal at stake: the old concept of the world. And as Galileo already experienced, the old does not give up all that easily, even when it becomes clear that the new functions.

In order to perceive angels we need another perspective. Yet, the rational mind tends to be in the way, which is why angel experiences are probably much more frequent in danger or death situations: the rational mind is blocked and switched off and we can perceive a reality beyond ourselves that we usually suppress. Then, as soon as the rational mind becomes active again, it naturally doubts these experiences.

Here is a brief description of my concept of the world. The following list is based on my own experiences and my own path. In addition to the basic assumptions, you will also find the views that have proved helpful in my life. You don't need to agree with it for this book to be of value to you. However, you can also make use of this book's perceptions and methods if you have another view of the world or a different attitude.

And one more thing: If the terms "God" or "the divine force"—which appear quite frequently in this book—bother you, simply replace them with something that seems right to you: origin, light, consciousness, unity, eternity, beginning and end, Great Spirit...

Basic Assumptions

- There is a spiritual world.
- There are angels, archangels, and a spiritual hierarchy.
- In the spiritual world, there are many beings who accompany and support humans on their spiritual path. We can come into contact with some of these beings. Among these are angels, archangels, and earthangels.
- There are other messengers and helpers in addition to the angels.
- The goal of human life is to develop, to consciously live in the earthly realm, and to once again remember the immortal, divine core of ourselves. We could even say that we want to overcome the duality in order to achieve unity. Others call it self-knowledge, perfection, enlightenment, awakening, finding our way to God, or returning to the origin.
- Not all human beings may have this goal. Some people may be incarnated with other tasks. Since my path is the path of becoming conscious, I base my life on it.
- There are many paths that lead to the goal—and the path described here is one of them.
- At the core of our being, we are whole. We already carry within us everything that we want to develop. Spiritual awakening means taking the veil from the light, once again remembering what is at the core of our being, and living consciously.
- Meditation, work with spiritual beings, angels, energetic tools, essences—all of these are paths for achieving the previously mentioned goal, but they are not an end in themselves.
- Each of us can create our lives through the creative force within us
- Each of us selects the learning field of duality, earthly life, our tasks in life, our parents, and the circumstances in which we grow up.
- Life can be fun—and it is also allowed to enjoy the process of freeing ourselves from the entanglements and to develop what is within us.

- Spirituality and everyday life are not separate. All of life serves spiritual development. Everyday life is usually the training field upon which we test whether our theories are right or whether we have truly understood and integrated our perceptions. And everyday life is one of the best mirrors for our inner lives.
- Everyday life shows whether we have assumed responsibility for our lives, whether we master everyday life or let ourselves be controlled by feelings, thoughts, and entanglements.
- The human being has a physical, a corporeal, and a subtle body. More information on this topic can be found in numerous books about the aura, the chakras, the energy system, or in the *LightBeings Master Essences* * book.
- In the subtle energy system, "becoming conscious" means dissolving blocks. This leads to becoming whole on all levels. Consequently, the body can also become healthy.
- Some energy forms and beings make their energy directly available to human beings. People can put it to use in meditation or even through directly energized essences.

How I Obtained the Information in this Book

I have personally experienced many of the things described in this book. I perceived other things during meditation or they became clear to me during conversations. We could call this "inspiration," information from the wordless voice inside of us. I had to examine this and clothe it in words. It appeared to me like a deep inner knowledge, to which I received access.

In addition, I was given numerous reports on experiences and feedback from other people who were involved in this topic or who had worked with the corresponding LightBeings Essences.

Two More Comments

We, Gerhard and Petra, have explored this topic and gathered experiences together. When you read "I" in this book, it will usually mean "we." Because the word "we" is used in this book as an expression for "we human beings," we have related our experiences in the "I" form. The meditations are written in the second-person form because this will make it easier for you to become involved in the images and energies and let yourself be moved by them.

---

* "LightBeings Master Essences" by Petra Schneider and Gerhard K. Pieroth, Arcana Publishing, Twin Lakes 1998

What If You Don't Believe?

Angel experiences do not occur through the rational mind, but on another level. Even the mystics who were involved with this topic describe them in this manner. However, if we still attempt to approach them in this way, the result is often something that doesn't really make sense. *Divyanand*[3] writes: "Organized religions generally have a confused view of angels because their theologians haven't experienced an encounter with them."

Today, recognizing the subtle, spiritual world is probably more difficult than during the age of Dionysius Areopagite *(shortly after Christ)* or Thomas of Aquinas *(around 1250 A.D.)*. In our current age, who trains the abilities for perceiving the spiritual world and the subtle energies? We don't learn this at school, we don't learn it from other people, and those who brought this gift with them as children have usually lost it. The inner voice, which has been suppressed by rational thinking and the *Enlightenment*, has become silent—or has the rational mind just become loud? But now the intuition is once again called for in areas other than the esoteric scene. Even in business life, in the "normal" world, the advantages of the intuition are gaining recognition. And so not only people involved in esoterics are training themselves to hear the inner voice, but also business people, physicians, and scientists. In the course of this training, many people also open up to the perception of subtle energies and beings. And the rational mind still doubts.

Will there ever be a resolution to this conflict with the rational mind? Even though I have already worked with the spiritual world for many years and have had a variety of experiences and much feedback, my rational mind does have its doubts time and again: "Am I just imagining this?" But now I place more emphasis on my experiences.

Although angels are mentioned in the Bible from the first book to the last as God's messengers, and the Archangels Gabriel, Michael, and Raphael are even named specifically, the Christian

Church also suppresses the angels. Rationalism, the *Enlightenment*, and materialism determine its concept of the world. The theologian Rudolf Bultmann has even said: "We cannot use electric lights and the radio, take advantage of the means of modern medicine, and believe in the world of spirits and wonders in the New Testament"[14].

Why not, I ask myself? Why is there a conflict between the spiritual world and the material world? Just because we consider a spiritual world to be real doesn't mean that we must push aside our logical minds. Just as our brain consists of two parts and the one side tends to work logically and the other tends to work intuitively, the world can also consist of a logically ascertainable side and an intuitively comprehensible aspect.

And haven't all the mystics of previous centuries—such as St. Hildegard of Bingen, Thomas of Aquinas, and Dionysius Areopagite—taught us that they have experienced this reality? Should we dismiss these individuals with their visions as dreamers and people out of touch with reality? These experiences are only unreal if we limit our definition of reality to the material, measurable world. But if we cannot perceive the spiritual world ourselves, how can we conclude that it does not exist? If an individual is red-green colorblind and cannot see these colors, should he conclude that these colors do not exist and everyone else who sees them is just imagining it? The stars also shine in the sky during the day. However, we do not see them because the light of the sun is too bright. And so we often do not hear the inner voice and the message of the angels because the rational mind is too loud.

Angels Through the Ages

In most religions and cultures, there are messengers between the divine force and human beings. It is their task to mediate between the people and the higher powers, as well as serving these higher powers. Although these beings don't always correspond with what we call angels, I would still like to present a brief survey of some of these mediators. They show that (almost) every culture and religion recognizes a spiritual world that accompanies the human beings and the divine force. We are familiar with the messengers of the gods from Greek mythology, such as Hermes, who reconciles and connects the differences between heaven and earth. There is also the winged female messenger of the gods, Iris, the rainbow goddess.

In the mythology of the Celts, there are no ascending and descending messengers because they don't have the upper world and underworld of the Greeks and Romans. The messengers of the gods were animals, frequently birds. Any animal could be a messenger from another world. The gods of the Celts lived on the earth and were anything but human. They dwelled in deep crevices, in the depths of the sea, in the heavens, and inside the mountains. They lived wherever the human being could not go. In addition to communicating through the animals, it was also possible for the human being to make direct contact with the gods[6].

In all of the high religions, we find messengers between the divine force and the human beings: The term "angel" comes from the Greek word *angelos*. *Seul*[13] writes that the image of the messenger gods was widespread in the entire Greek and Roman region. Angels and demons were depicted here as the forces that move the cosmos. The early Jewish and rabbinical concepts of the Apocrypha, Qumran, Talmud, and mysticism form the foundation of the Jewish belief in angels. And, in the same vein, the first (Ethiopian) Enoch book was revealed by the angels. It was created in 150 B.C.[14]

The Bible *(Acts of the Apostles 23)* reports that there were conflicting views of angels even during the age of Jesus. The Sadducees—the religious party in Judaism that consisted of high-ranking priests and worldly aristocrats—denied the existence of angels, spirits, and the resurrection. But the Pharisees (the other strong religious party) taught that they did exist.

However, these weren't the first statements about messenger beings. Even the most ancient oriental high religion of Sumer is filled with divine spirit beings who ascend and descend from the heavens. They were sent by the deities to communicate their will to the human beings, to bring aid or ruin, to develop living things, to reward, and to punish. So the Babylonians and Assyrians were also familiar with good spirits and convinced that every human being has a protecting spirit. These spirits were depicted with wings in the art of the ancient Orient, Greece, and Rome. They are often mixed beings, part human and part animal. Illustrations on a consecrated water basin belonging to the Sumerian King Gueda from the period around 2600 B.C. show the hovering protecting spirits administering heavenly water to the king.

In the religions of Sumer, Babylon, and Assyria, we also find the Kerub, the massive, solemn protective spirits. They are the guardians of the heavenly and earthly shrines, mediators between the worlds, and interceders for the human beings to the great gods. They are portrayed as powerful winged human figures, but sometimes also as winged mixed beings with human and animal elements. They are considered to be the oldest portrayals of angels and the models for the Jewish and Christian seraphim[13].

Just like Moses, Elijah, Isaiah, Daniel, and later Mohammed, Zarathustra—the founder of Parseeism—also received a vision: He looked into the spiritual world and heard the voice of the angel. The angel gave him the divine message that he was to pass on to human beings.

In the holy writings of Hinduism, the angels are called *devas*. They increase the consciousness of the soul and therefore bring cheerfulness, joy, beauty, love, serenity, carefreeness, and fear-lessness[3].

The spiritual helpers in Tibetan Buddhism are called *dakinis*—heaven-runners. They bring messages and advice, make prophecies, as well as warning, protecting, and inspiring human beings. However, they do not correspond to the angels of the Western tradition[14].

The belief in angels is a solid component of Islam. The messengers are called *malaika*, a word that appears more than 80 times in the Koran. The Koran itself is believed to have been dictated to the Prophet Mohammed by the angel Gabriel. These messengers are connected with various human activities, with all of the occurrences in life and in nature, and are considered the "treasurers and administrators of divine grace." Gabriel, Michael, and Azazil (also Izrail—Angel of Death) are mentioned by name[9]. In addition, there are guardian angels, protecting angels, and death angels[14].

In the Bible

Angels appear in the Bible from the very beginning: The cherubim guarded the Garden of Eden as well as the path to the Tree of Life with flaming, flashing swords, after Adam and Eve were forced to leave Paradise *(Genesis 3:24)*; the angels of the Lord give advice and announce progeny (in *Genesis 16*, they appear to Hagar, Abraham's beloved) and save people in distress: Lot is rescued from the destruction of Sodom and Gomorra *(Genesis 19)*, an angel rescues Hagar and her son after Abraham drove them away *(Genesis 21: 17-18)*, and an angel rescues Abraham's son from the fire sacrifice *(Genesis 22)*.

And that isn't all. Angels are mentioned in many places in the Bible, from the first book of the Old Testament to the last book of the New Testament. And they are not just minor figures, but also intervene in earthly occurrences. They are heralds, bringing and interpreting visions. They appear in dreams, warn people, and give explanations. They challenge people to do something, and they free people from imprisonment.

Each of the four evangelists speaks about angels or reports that Jesus spoke about angels. Here are some examples: *John 20:12* and the subsequent text reports that two angels in white garments sat in Jesus' grave; John, Matthew, and Mark describe how Jesus mentioned angels in his speeches about the last days *(Matthew 16:27, 24:31, 24:36, 25:31; Mark 20:12* and following) and in parables *(John 1:51, Mark 12:25, Matthew 13:39, 18:10)*. *Luke 1:11-38* describes how the archangel Gabriel announced the birth of John the Baptist and of Jesus, as well as how Jesus spoke of the angels of God *(Luke 11:8-9, 15:10, 16:22)*.

The term "archangel" is also used in the Bible: In *the First Letter of Paul to the Thessalonians*, he writes "For the Lord himself will descend from heaven with a cry of command, with the archangel's call, and with the sound of the trumpet of God." *1st Thessalonians 4:16*. The archangel Michael, who fought with the Devil, is mentioned by Jude in his letter *(Jude 9)*.

In the Old Testament, the name Prince of Angels is also used. This means angels who lead an entire nation.

Angels in Other Writings

Probably the most fundamental writing of Christianity about angels comes from Dionysius Areopagite. Around 500 A.D., a secret teaching that focused on the heavenly hierarchies and angelic beings appeared in publication under his name. The author wrote that the origin of the teaching can be traced back to Dionysius Areopagite, a student of the apostle Paul. Paul initiated Dionysius Areopagite, who gained his perceptions through "inspirations" on the path of initiation.

Even today, scholars argue whether the author actually was a student of the apostle Paul, who is also mentioned in the Bible

(Acts of the Apostles 17:34) and why a secret teaching was suddenly written down. The rejection of mysticism began around the time that this teaching was put into writing. Between 300 and 500 A.D., the mystery schools were closed and destroyed. People distanced themselves increasingly from consciousness and the path of initiation. Faith took the place of contemplation and inner perception. Initiation and enlightenment were suppressed by dogma, which had to be supported by the authority of the church[12].

Today many people are taking this path in the opposite direction. Dionysius Areopagite has once again become modern. However, through the ages his writings have always inspired people like Bernhard of Clairveaux, Pope Gregory the Great, Hildegard of Bingen, Bonaventura, Thomas of Aquinas, and Rudolph Steiner.

Angels Today: Powerful Partners?

"We are not the light, we are not the message. We are the messengers." (from *Faraway, So Close!* a film by Wim Wenders)

The word "angel" is derived from the Greek term *angelos*, which means "messenger" or "envoy." Angels are the messengers of the divine. As described in the chapter on "Angels in Various Religions and Cultures," these messengers can be found in many cultures. Yet, this usually doesn't mean angels as we understand them today. When I speak of angels, archangels, or earthangels in this book, I mean spiritual beings who work on realizing the divine plan and never have left the consciousness of unity. They have never been incarnated and never experienced the veil of forgetting.

Another explanation of the word "angel" is derived from ancient Egyptian: *ang* means "life" and *el* means "God's light." So angels are those who "live in the light of God."

In the Spiritual Hierarchy

When people first become interested in the spiritual world, they think that there is a hopeless chaos. We hear of angels, archangels, cherubim, ascended masters, Metatron, devas, nature spirits, astral beings, and souls. I needed some time to find the order involved here. Yet, this order does exist and it isn't new. For many centuries now, it has been called the spiritual or heavenly hierarchy.

We shouldn't imagine this hierarchy to be like a dictatorship: God, the ruler, sits on the throne above everything else and gives orders and commands. Beneath him are the archangels and angels, who must carry out these commands like silent servants or machines. A more appropriate metaphor for this would be the model of a democratically organized, ideal company. The "head" is the executive board, which possesses the most extensive vision and the greatest understanding. This is why it presents ideas, gives impulses, and shows others the direction. If this is an automotive company, for example, it decides to put something new on the market. This impulse is then passed on to the department heads or managers, who then meet with their employees and make specific plans. After a number of concrete steps, the order reaches the workers, who then build the new car.

Every level has its tasks. The levels of the spiritual hierarchy are differentiated from each other by their degree of consciousness, their vibrational level, and their closeness to unity. The hierarchy of the spiritual world is not built upon power, but upon the degree of consiousness or closeness to unity, to the origin. The unity, the origin, or God is all embracing. Although God is at the tip of the spiritual hierarchy, this is actually depicted falsely since God includes everything. If we put him at the top, he becomes limited. Since the creating impulses come from God, he still forms the tip of the hierarchy (see illustration on p. 28). Two rays with differing orientations emerge from the unity:

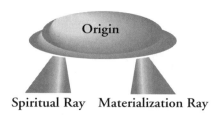

Spiritual Ray   Materialization Ray

The Spiritual Ray

The beings of the spiritual ray are responsible for the spiritual aspect of the Creation. They create a spiritual learning field and accompany other beings on the path of increasing consciousness. Among these spiritual beings are Metatron, the archangels, the angels, and the ascended masters.

The Materialization Ray

The beings of this ray bring the divine impulses into more condensed forms and into the material aspect of the Creation. These includes, for examples, the order of Melchizedek, the earthangels, nature angels, nature spirits, and devas.

There is naturally no strict separation between these two rays. They both work together and ultimately serve both rays of the Creation, the play of the cosmos. This situation is best illustrated by the image of two interlinking spirals. They bring form to the divine impulse and they also dissolve the forms.

At the tip of the ray are the beings closest to the origin, to God, to the unity. They receive the impulse of the divine force and pass it on to subsequent levels until it is ultimately translated into action. The further "down" they are on this ray, meaning the closer they get to duality, the less vision and consciousness the beings possess.

This description is a model upon which we can orient our human minds and with which we can explain and understand many things. However, we human beings with our dual way of thinking are hardly capable of comprehending what "reality" actually looks like.

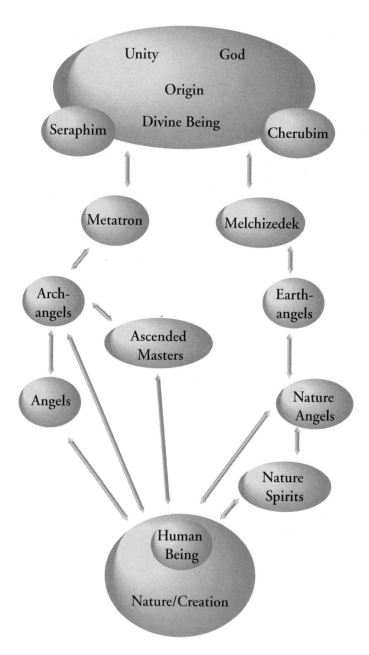

The spiritual hierarchy

Archangels and Angels

Archangels are at the top of the angel hierarchy, which is also illustrated by their name: the Greek word *archein* means "to be the first, stand at the top, to rule."[13]

Archangels are creations of unity. They are not the origin. To the same degree, they are not in the origin, in the one, in the all-embracing, in the void. Archangels are not God since they are already differentiated and no longer everything or all-embracing. This is also shown by their names, which end in *el*: Michael, Gabriel, Zadkiel, etc. This Hebraic ending means "like God," "of God," "representing God." (For more about Metatron, see page 108, The archangels are like colored light that, even if it has just a shimmer of a color, is already different from white light. They are individual, even if they are still very close to the origin.

The essential difference between them and human beings is that the angels have always existed in the consciousness of unity and that they do never incarnated the duality or polarity. Exceptions to this are Metatron and Melchiezdek (see respective sections). Angels are in oneness, which we could also call non-polarity or unipolarity. This one pole is outside of the duality in which we live. The following pictures illustrates this concept:

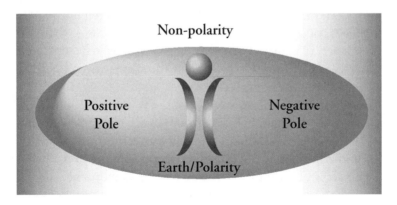

Polarity and non-polarity

Furthermore, the archangels have no material bodies. They are not even part of the subtle realm. They are like thoughts, like light, but not material. Yet, they possess the ability of materializing, which means they can become visible to us.

Since angels have no material bodies, they are not subject to the laws of matter. They can move freely through time and space. Perhaps this is what the wings symbolize. Since angels do not need to obey earthly laws, it is easy for them to perform "miracles." What else are miracles than occurrences that do not correspond to earthly possibilities or laws?

Earthly reality is duality. Our life moves between two poles, which are also called "good" and "evil." The tension between good and evil is our training field within which we progress. Even if we only do good and fight evil, we still remain within the tension between the poles. "Evil" continues to be part of our life. It is even necessary in order for us to fight against it and be able to do good. The poles serve us in recognizing "good and evil" and having the free choice. There is no choice without the poles.

Adam and Eve lived in Paradise, in unity. For them there was no tension between poles and no choice. There was just one pole. Only after they ate from the tree of knowledge, when they had internalized the fruit of knowledge, were they capable of recognizing good and evil. But they could no longer see the unity. They had lost paradise. The tension between the poles is the motor of cognition and our training field. This is where we experience, in pain and suffering, what it means to be separated from the unity, from God. And, at the same time, all beauty, love, and happiness remind us of our origin.

The further we move away from the positive pole into evil, the stronger the longing that draws us back. How many people reach the spiritual path and begin to search for the meaning of life and a fulfilled life because of suffering and painful experiences? It is often the negative pole—the "unpleasant" side of life—that sets us into motion. The further we distance ourselves from the positive pole, the greater the tension will be. At the same time, the strength to once again move toward the positive will also be more intense.

The positive pole is still in the tension of duality. When people fight against evil and want to lock it out of their lives, they continue to maintain the duality. Redemption occurs when things are brought together. This is also emphasized by the name of the negative pole—*Diabolus*. *Diabolus* comes from "dividing" and "separating"—and as long as these poles are separated, there will be tension. It is only when we bring them together within us that they can merge and vanish. This means that we must also look at our own shadow aspects in order to release them—as Christ has taught us—and thereby move toward a position outside of the duality. If we succeed in liberating ourselves from this duality, from this classification, then we are free and outside of the poles. Then we are in the non-polar realm, which is also called enlightenment or awakening.

Achieving this point of view does not mean giving up the body and existing outside of earthly life. It is an internal work, an inner standpoint, that we can also experience in moments of meditation and bliss. We usually fall out of it again.

Archangels are therefore beyond duality. They perceive the meaning and correlation and do not judge. "It is as it is, neither good nor evil, neither wrong nor right." They recognize that tension is a wonderful training field, that experiences are possible here that are not possible in the oneness. Here is the possibility of departing ourselves from "God" and then returning to him again. In the duality, we can experience what it means to be separated from God, separated from oneness, and even forget that we were ever in the unity and a part of the divine nature. We can even feel this with all of our senses through our human body, but we can feel the opposite as well. We immerse ourselves in forgetting in order to consciously remember.

Since angels are outside of the duality, they are also sexless. There are no feminine or masculine angels. However, their energy can tend to be feminine, nurturing, and gentle like

Chamuel or masculine and powerfully strong like that of the archangel Michael.

The angels and many other beings of the spiritual world, like the ascended masters, live outside the duality, in non-polarity. They are in a state of oneness.

Yet, the state of oneness is not just one uniform state. There are many different degrees of consciousness here, as shown in the next illustration:

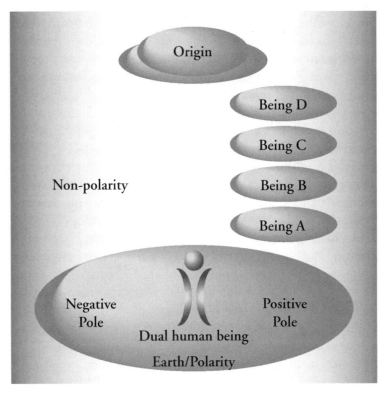

Different degrees of consciousness in the state of oneness

The beings A to D are distinguished by their closeness to the origin and their degree of consciousness. A could be the consciousness of a human being who has overcome the duality and remain in a human body (enlightened individuals). But it is still close to the duality. Being B represents an angel. Being C could be an ascended master, and D could be an archangel.

Just as human beings possess auras of varying density (from the subtly vibrating spiritual bodies to the dense ether bodies), archangels also extend over various spheres of vibrations. One portion of their being is close to the origin, and the other portion is close to the earth. Archangels are the connection between origin and duality. They connect these two levels like a bridge. We can use the example of color to illustrate this: When archangels are in the upper vibrational area, they are close to unity and almost white. The closer their vibrations are to the earth, the more intensive their color will be. For example, the energy of Michael is white close to the origin with a touch of light blue; the closer we get to the portion that is near the earth, the more intense the blue becomes. This portion is also depicted as a royal-blue warrior with a flaming sword.

Archangels are the bridge between unity (origin) and duality (earth)

When we make contact with the archangels, we can become immersed in various levels. What vibrational level of the archangel we reach depends upon our own degree of development, as well as the topic with which we approach the angel.

Archangels are very powerful and strong. We human beings presumably cannot bear their total strength, their high vibrational level, and their bright light. Our energy system would probably vibrate too intensively and lose its stability in a direct encounter with the archangel. This is also expressed in the Bible. When the archangels appear, their first words are usually: "Fear not." When the archangel Gabriel appeared to the seer Daniel, Daniel lost consciousness *(Daniel 8)*. When archangels come into contact with human beings or when we invite them to, they usually adapt their light and their vibration to us. Then there isn't such vehement physical reaction. In many places in the Bible, there are descriptions of how angels appeared in the form of men and were only recognized as angels later.

Archangels and angels appear in a form that we can comprehend. They manifest themselves in the form of someone who we can accept and trust. This is probably why there are also various portrayals and images of archangels: as light, as human figures, with and without wings.

Archangels are like prisms that split the white light of unity into various colors. By doing so, they make it possible for us to experience the white light. Dionysius Areopagite called the angels "proclaimers." They are the first to register the divine impulses and then "report" them to us so that we can understand them. They reflect the aspects of God and the "formless" is conveyed "through form" by way of the angels[12].

Archangels represent various aspects of God, just as the 99 Names of God in Islam depict different aspects or principles of the nameless, the all-embracing. Chamuel represents the principle of divine love; Michael stands for divine willpower; through Uriel we learn to turn divine vision into reality. We could even call archangels "interpreters": they make the divine understandable to human beings. And they help people recognize and develop the various aspects of the divine within themselves.

Angels are the "staff" of the archangels. They are closer to the earth than the archangels and are also not as powerful. Many people feel more familiar with them. They also appear more frequently than archangels. There are a multitude of angels with various tasks: the angels of healing, the angels of joy, the angels of wisdom, the angels of relationships, the angels of patience—just to name a few.

There are also implementing angels on the materialization ray. In order to differentiate between them, we can use the name of nature angels for the angels of the materialization ray (also see Illustration, "The spiritual hierarchy", pag. 28).

Even if the angels are not on the same level as the archangels, they are still powerful beings. The pictures of angels as sweet, cute fluttery winged creatures focus on the playfulness and child-like innocence of angels, not showing their power. Angels also possess abilities and possibilities that exceed the human ability of imagination.

As long as they exist within the unity, angels don't use their free will. This doesn't mean that they have no will. As long as they are in the unity they are completely in harmony with the divine will. Angels can leave the unity to enter the duality and become human beings.

Guardian Angels

Guardian angels are the angels who personally stand at our side. They are individual companions and protectors for *one* human being. Like all angels, the guardian angels are very powerful and can work in various ways. Since they are at home on the spiritual ray, they mainly focus on our development. They support us in fulfilling our own life plan. This is why they may even allow accidents or mishaps to occur because it could be precisely what is required to trigger the next growth step. Even if we have doubts about our guardian angels or do not perceive them, they stand at our side. They can only intercede if this act is part of the cosmic plan.

We can choose whether we learn our lessons through suffering or in a pleasant way. Guardian angels can help us perceive this lesson more quickly and create favorable circumstances so that our life becomes more enjoyable. But we must request this of them.

Different Angels—Different Roles

Specific Tasks of Archangels

Although archangels do not exist within the duality, they have an effect here and can therefore be perceived. We can compare this to how the sun is not here on the earth but its rays still warm our planet.

Archangels are "bridge angels." They create a link between the divine force and the earthly-material world, between the Creator and the Creation. And like the arch of a bridge, they connect in both directions, from the unity and to the unity. They not only serve human beings—which is just *one* aspect of their tasks—but also the entire Creation.

The tasks of the archangels are:

1) Translating divine impulses into action. In this way they participate in the creation process.
2) Making it possible God to be experienced.
3) Accompanying human beings on the path back to the unity.

Archangels Translate Divine Impulses into Action

Archangels and angels participate in the creation process. The archangels receive the impulses of the divine force and transform them "downward." In order for matter to be produced from the non-material impulse, it must be condensed into energy, into particles, and ultimately into compact matter. Just as the thought of a house does not mean that the house will be created as a result, there are many steps in between—making the thought visible through plans, producing the material, joining the material together into form, equipping and decorating the shell of the house—there are also many intermediate steps between the Creator's impulse and the Creation. And this task is assumed by the entire spiritual world. The archangels, who receive the thoughts and pass them on to the angels, can be compared to transformers. In this process, it does not matter whether the goal is to create planets and galaxies, the earth, animals or humans, or specific situations.

I think that the angels do not create galaxies in the way that children build sandcastles. They do not assemble the atoms in order to form suns and planets. The angels give the impulses, the impetus, the energy—and this is what causes the reactions to occur. They give the impulse so that the supernova explodes and a new solar system is created as a result. They give the impulse so that the cloud of gas contracts and a new planet is formed from it. They give the impulse so that a "primeval soup" of organic molecules appears and then gives further impulses for organisms, living creatures, and human beings.

This is how the archangels and angels bring the spiritual impulses and principles into reality, into our earthly reality and the reality of other planets and systems. As a result, they fulfill their messenger function. At the same time, they maintain the divine order and give regulating impulses when processes deviate from the order.

Archangels Make It Possible for Us to Experience God

White light is difficult to describe. All colors are contained within white light, just as everything is contained within God. All religions of the earth express that our human mind is not capable of comprehending God or understanding the entire nature of God. Yet, it is our goal, the goal of our soul, to experience God and return to the unity. This is the goal of all religions. And the archangels serve this goal. This means that they are important helpers on the path to enlightenment, to the experience of God, to experience of the SELF, to the light, or whatever we may call it.

The archangels make it possible for us to experience God. Like a prism divides white light into many colors, the archangels reflect the various aspects of God. They are like the prism. They absorb the white light and each archangel contains the entire spectrum of colors. Yet, they then intensify one aspect of this spectrum so that we human beings can experience and comprehend this aspect. For example, Michael intensifies the aspect of the divine will (color blue), Raphael the aspect of divine healing (color green). They not only do this for human beings but also within the entire creation.

The various archangels represent different aspects of God or, as it is also called, "principles of the divine." This is one aspect.

The other aspect is: They help people comprehend the various facets of God. Thomas of Aquinas said that the angels are pure, clear mirrors of the divine. But this divine light is weak in human beings[5]. We have distanced ourselves further from the divine force than the archangels have. Our mirror is no longer so close to the source of the light and the veils of forgetting prevent it from powerfully reflecting the divine light. On the path of rediscovering the divine, the archangels help us on the one hand by letting the light shine more intensely on the mirror, strengthening the divine spark within us so that we also perceive it. On the other hand, they pull the veil away little by little, dissolving blocks in the energy system.

Light is the symbol of consciousness. The archangels are completely conscious, but we are not. Consequently, the archangels and angels intensify our consciousness so that we can once again recognize the divine. This recognition does not occur through the rational mind. The dual mind cannot understand unity. This recognition occurs on another level, which we can call intuition, deep perception, or mystical experience. It does not appear in words because words are the tools of the mind. We receive this insight in silence. Thomas of Aquinas said that angels proclaim the divine silence. Voiceless concepts of heart or thought are born in silence[5]. In stillness, in meditation, we come into harmony with divine silence, go into resonance, and receive the insight. The next step is then to accept this on the level of the mind, and the archangels help in this process. They are the "bringers of insight or wisdom" for the mind and spirit.

Archangels Guide Us on the Path to Becoming Conscious

Since archangels are close to unity, it is easy for them to recognize the divine core of our being. They do not allow themselves to be deceived by our masks, behavior patterns, feelings, entanglements, or self-image. They strengthen our true being so that we can also experience, sense, and recognize it. They pull away the veil so that we can remember and develop our true being. They bring messages in the form of visions, occurrences, encounters, and other "coincidences" so that we can wake up. And they also help us to understand these just like Gabriel was sent to the seer Daniel in order to interpret his visions *(The Bible, Daniel 8 and 9)*.

Archangels and angels are our companions on the path of forgetting. When our soul makes the decision to learn on the earth through incarnations, the veil of forgetting drops over our consciousness. We forget who we really are. We forget our light. Yet, we remain light, even if we have greatly distanced ourselves from the divine force, even if we become entangled with the dark pole. The divine spark lives within us, even if we do not see it. This is the path of becoming conscious: We forget and re-member bit by bit, just like we sometimes wake up in the morning with a fragment of a dream and then arduously draw this dream out of our forgetting, piece by piece.

The work with the archangels involves awakening consciousness. This is their goal and our task. We are meant to remember our divine being, that we are part of the divine. The work with the archangels is concerned with consciousness—not living through situations one more time or painfully suffering through something. Archangels bring us the gift of grace: "Speak but one word and your sins shall be forgiven."

We no longer must atone for our mistakes. We no longer must arduously transform what separates us, what blocks us. We no longer must clear our karma. As opposed to the usual transformation work, the archangel can take away the veil when we have recognized which veil darkens our light and are will-ing to let go of it. This is also described in the Bible when the prophet Isaiah sees God and his angels in a vision. Isaiah recognizes that he is impure. One of the seraphim flies down to him, touches him with a glowing coal and says: "...your guilt is taken away, and your sin is forgiven." And Isaiah be-comes pure.

However, this deals with more than just recognizing and understanding. It also does not ultimately imply always calling on Michael for protection and strength or requesting Raphael's help in every case of healing. Archangels invite us to develop this aspect of the divine force within ourselves: awakening "Michael" within us and becoming "Raphael" and completely healed. We want to reawaken to divine existence, together with all the aspects and qualities that have been given to us on the path. The archangels accompany us so that we can develop these qualities within us and live in the body, in the earthly duality.

Archangels and angels are always at our side, no matter whether we perceive them or not. They accompany us, even when they do not intervene. They allow us our free will, accept our decisions and the path that we choose. Since they do not judge the pain and suffering of duality as being bad, it is also easy for them to see the positive aspects of this path. They recognize that the human being must experience the dark side to once again see the light. They know that we must undergo unpleasant experiences so that we start searching for the light. And they accompany us on the entire path, even when we immerse ourselves in the negative pole.

In some books or teachings it is said that the angels only accompany us as long as we are on the path to God. I even read: "The Christian loses his guardian angel because of sin" [14]. Or that the angels turn away as soon as we follow the path into the darkness. This is nonsense. The learning field of duality was created by God so that we become conscious, so that we recognize what it means to be in God or separated from him. And he has given us free will. Our soul learns through every experience. And God's love accompanies us on the entire path. What would free will be if we were not allowed to use it, if God would take the angels away from us as soon as we chose a path that leads away from him?

In the biblical story of the lost son, which also illustrates what it means to leave the unity (also see page 111), the father gives the son his portion of the inheritance, even though the son leaves him. The father knows that this son must have experiences in order to recognize what he is giving up. Jesus expresses the same thing in his parable of the lost sheep: "...he rejoices over (the found sheep) more than over the ninety-nine that never went astray."

Angels and archangels never leave us. They are at our side, and the moment we ask them for help, we receive it, no matter how "evil" we are. We also do not need to first reach a certain level of development or have the proper attitude, as some people have written. Our request and our willingness are enough. However, it is necessary for us to ask and be willing.

How Archangels Work

The power of the archangels connects us with the core of our being, with the divine nature within us. So we can perceive who we truly are, which abilities and possibilities we possess, and what we want to develop. And we can recognize what stops us from doing so. These blocks hang like veils in front of the light. Archangels have the ability of simply taking away these veils by raising our vibration.

Our emotional and mental/spiritual state is determined by various vibrational areas. If the vibrational level of a human being is extremely low, he will feel dull, heavy, and stuck in emotions and behavior patterns. His aura layers are so strongly condensed that there is hardly any energy flowing. People with a high vibrational level have developed spiritual consciousness and are in an emotionally stable state. They feel joyful, confident, and happy—no matter what happens. When the energy level falls, we once again get stuck in a "hole," in our negative feelings, old patterns, and thought structures.

The power of the archangels raises us out of the lower vibrational areas to a higher level and stabilizes this state. They lift us out of the old patterns, and we can behave differently than we normally would have. The only thing we need to do is ask since even archangels are not permitted to help if we do not ask for it. But when we ask them, their power is enormous.

I experienced this at one point when I sat in a "hole." Gerhard and I had quarrel because I had once again spread myself out and had taken away his space. I fell into the old pattern of "I'm not allowed to live my power because I will otherwise get into trouble. But if I don't live it, I don't feel well. It's a hopeless situation." Depressed and annoyed, I stewed. I couldn't see any way out of the situation and, as often before, didn't see any meaning in life. Then I had a thought: "You could ask the archangels to help you." "Why," countered another inner voice, "what should they do since there is no way out of this situation, there is no solution." "But just try it," said the first voice. "No, there's no sense in it. They can't do anything because there's no way out." I observed the inner dialog and noticed how I angrily clung to my situation and my despair. I was not willing to move on. Yet, I had a defiant thought: "Ok, I'll try it. Archangels, please help me—even if I know that you can't find any solution." I was not willing, clung to my mood, and continued turning on my pessimistic carousel of thoughts.

However, I was surprised to discover that my feelings became lighter. I began to smile at myself, and this pessimistic mood disappeared within 15 minutes later. It simply dissolved away, even though I didn't do anything and even though I held onto it so desperately. When Gerhard arrived, we were able to calmly talk about it and were each able to think about our own contribution. Of course, there a way out—and it involved both of us.

What had happened in the situation described above? I had gotten stuck on a low energy level at first and also wasn't willing to do something about it. Through the request, and despite the resistance, the archangels had raised my vibrational level and freed me from the swamp of my negative feelings. And I was able to see and think clearly again, recognizing the possibilities.

It is easy for archangels to lift us out of entanglements. However, it is often difficult for us to deal with this occurrence. Our old patterns and problems suddenly disappear and yet we still don't have a new behavior for the improved inner state. In earlier times, I couldn't believe that this could be a problem. However, I have often experienced that people have a hard time dealing with things when they change suddenly, when they have made a leap and suddenly find themselves in another place. This is why some people have an easier time working with methods that lead them step by step, like the ascended masters do.

Angels are experts in miracles—and their work often appears to us to be a miracle. Consequently, the chapter on "Creating a Partnership" (see page 59 ff.) also describes that we should "hand over." But be aware that it may be difficult to let go of old habits. And sometimes we go back to them again.

Archangels raise us up to a vibrational level that is viable for us. They do not bring us into a state that we cannot deal with or that would be too intense for us. Through their power, we sometimes experience states in which we feel completely well and at home—and then these states disappear again and we are confronted with our old modes of behavior. This is also one of their work methods. We can only develop certain states, certain qualities of our being, when we have experienced them ourselves. And so the archangels make it easier for us to have this experience and the path there becomes easier.

Through the support of the archangels we can more easily, pleasantly, and quickly take the path of becoming conscious, the path into oneness, the path to a fulfilled life. But we have to—or better yet, *are allowed to*—walk it ourselves.

Tasks of the Angels

As already described, angels are the "workers" who carry out the tasks together with the archangels. They are experts who have specialized in one field. For example, Raphael works with the angels of healing. If we ask Raphael for healing, he brings us into harmony with the soul plan and the learning step, while the angels of healing are concerned with the feelings and the body. There are a great many angels for the multitude of tasks and aspects. Angels also have the ability to increase the vibration. Sometimes angels touch us and we suddenly feel joy, hope, and peace within ourselves. This was also depicted in the *Wings of Desire* film by Wim Wenders. Pessimistic thoughts or despair give way to hope when people are touched by an angel. Angels make it possible for us to have certain experiences and offer us their help. Whether or not we use this offer depends on us.

Earthangels and Nature Angels

Earthangels are the archangels of the materialization ray. Just as the archangels translate the aspects and principles of the divine force in the spiritual realm, the earthangels bring them into form and materiality. They also connect the divine with the earthly. However, they translate the divine impulse into the material realm of the Creation and enable us to experience it there.

The tasks of the earthangels are:

1) Bringing the divine impulses into the material creation.
2) Bringing material and spirit into harmony.
3) Making it possible to experience the Creator through the Creation.

Earthangels Bring the Divine Impulses into the Material Creation

Earthangels also receive the impulses of the divine and transform them in a downward direction. They condense the impulses so that these become embodied in the material world. They develop and form the Creation. They work together with the angels of nature who, like the angels, are the "workers." In turn, the nature angels are interwoven with the nature spirits: the devas, elves, dwarfs, gnomes, etc.

Earthangels and archangels work hand in hand. Just as the physical body is connected with the subtle bodies and the mind in the human being, every material creation is interwoven with the spiritual essence.

Earthangels and archangels, angels and nature angels—all of these work together in turning the divine plan into reality, in creating the universe, the galaxies, and planets, the earth, the plants, and human beings. They intervene to regulate the situation when the Creation deviates from the divine plan.

Earthangels Bring Matter and Spirit into Harmony

As depicted in illustration on page 28, Melchizedek stands at the top of the materialization ray. Melchizedek (also see page 137 ff.) is the priest king. He brings the spiritual consciousness into the material world and everyday life. Consequently, the materialization ray involves not only pure materialization, but also the condensation of vibration into matter. All matter is created from spirit. And spirit, the divine, wants to express itself in the material world, in everyday life.

So the earthangels have a contributing effect on consciousness. In the same way that the archangels support human beings, they also help the creatures of nature to continuously develop their consciousness. Every existence that has been created strives toward higher development. The earthangels and the nature angels are companions and carry the divine principle into matter. They are also concerned with themes like "connecting heaven and earth," "expressing the divine," "will and assertion," and "healing." The Earthangel Sun embodies the principle of expressing the divine light through physical beauty. The Earthangel Tree brings the cosmic and earthly energies into harmony.

We shouldn't just seek the effects of these angels in dense matter—the subtle world is also material. The angels of the materialization ray accompany the subtle creatures of nature like elves, fairies, and gnomes and are responsible for their further development, for their "advancement." And they work in the subtle areas of the material creation—in crystals, trees, and animals. They also accompany these creations in creating harmony with the divine and continuing their development. But they also have an effect on human beings. They are the guardians of the human body and effect the subtle areas of the aura. They harmonize the flow of energy and enable us to develop and embody the qualities of the soul. They support us in translating our soul plan into reality, expressing our emotional qualities, and living the perfection of our divine spark in the earthly realm. They connect the body and the soul. Our body shapes itself according to our abilities and tasks. This forms the basis for physiognomy and palm reading.

Earthangels Make It Possible to Experience the Creator Through the Creation

Just like the archangels, the earthangels also make it possible for us to experience God—through the material world and nature. They bring the love and beauty of God into the forms, colors, and fragrances that touch us. Through a sunset, we can enter into a place of stillness and feel unity. The song of the birds can enchant us so that we forget our worries and experience joy. On the top of a mountain, we feel liberated from the heaviness of earthly existence and open up to the voice of our soul. We are moved by nature. We can discover and sense our own identity when we are out in the countryside. The earthangels connect us with God through nature and the material world.

Nature angels work together with human beings in the shamanic realm. They intensify its rituals so that energies and forces are set in motion and the vibrations and power are strengthened. These are better known in the natural religions or shamanic culture than in the Christian tradition, but with different names. Perhaps you are asking why the earthangels have been mentioned so rarely in literature. Why have the archangels been familiar to us for centuries, but not the earthangels? There are two reasons for this:

Up to Now, the Spiritual and Material Realms Have Been Considered to be Separate

There are many people who have been interested in the nature spirits and the materialization ray, but without seeing their connection with the spiritual ray. Or they have perceived the connection, the cooperation, to be a unity and have not described them separately.

The spirits and forces of nature are known to all cultures. They have frequently been worshipped as gods. For example, the tree or the evergreen world ash tree Yggdrasil of Nordic mythology is seen as an expression of the earthangel that connects heaven and earth. The same can be said for the sun, which is worshipped by many native peoples and was worshipped by the early advanced cultures. It embodies the light. Earthangels have been called upon and involved in matters related to food, hunting, or sun and rain for the growth of the plants. "Thanksgiving" is ultimately acknowledgment for this aspect of God.

In our Western culture, the area of nature spirits has been suppressed. When Christianity spread, there was *one* God who stood above everything else. Since the so-called heathen cultures also worshipped the divine aspects in nature, the nature gods were seen as competition for the one God and fought against. As a result, they were not permitted their continued existence as aspects of the divine. In order to overthrow the old beliefs, all other gods had to be destroyed. And this meant that the nature angels and earthangels were condemned as heathen in the Western world. They were ultimately suppressed from consciousness, plunged into the darkness of forgetting.

The Earthangels Have a Stronger Effect on Human Beings Today

In our current age, human consciousness has reached a level that it has not had for centuries. Although it is certain that there have been individual people time and again who have developed their divine being and attained perfect consciousness, they have been the exception. The broad masses have struggled with survival and have had little time for spiritual development.

Today, increasingly more people are walking the spiritual path. Consequently, collective consciousness is also being raised. Concepts and topics that were accessible to very few individuals in earlier times—the secret teachings—are published in many books today. The path has become more accessible and easier. And many spiritual helpers aid us on this path. So the earthangels now also have a strong effect on human beings, supporting us on the material side in increasing our consciousness. Just like the archangels accompany our spiritual development, the earthangels and their companions on the material and subtle planes create the possibility of making a leap in consciousness.

One further comment on the names: We received the earthangel names that we use in this book during meditation. During this time, they came to us as energies. They are a description of their qualities, which is why they aren't "ancient names." However, there are old names for these principles and for these angels like Nothanael. But since I have not spent my time researching the history of the earthangels, I am not familiar with them.

The Hierarchy of the Materialization Ray

The hierarchy of the materialization ray is depicted in the illustration, page 28. Melchizedek stands at the top, with the earthangels and nature angels below. Within the earthangels, Crystal, Sun, and Tree embody the more highly organized principles. The earthangels of the four elements are not the elements themselves. For example, the names do not refer to the element of air, but to the divine principle of the air element. This principle is the easiness, quickness, and flexibility embodied by the air element. The four element earthangels are portrayed as the bull (or Taurus, principle of earth), eagle (also the Scorpio, principle of water), lion (or Leo, principle of fire), and angel or human being as the principle of air. These principles are still used in astrology today.

The earthangels of the four elements are higher angels who let the impulses flow to the appropriate nature angels, to the nature spirits, and then into the elements. This means that earthangels are not the forces with which magic, shamanism, or people in past centuries have worked. They are the balanced creative aspects of these qualities, which bring us into harmony with these forces. They teach us how to use these forces in order to develop ourselves and become complete. They teach us the joy of creation through the elemental forces.

The angels of the four elements work together with the nature spirits: The angel of the earth works with the so-called little people, the dwarfs, imps, fairies, gnomes, and elves. The angel of the air is associated with the sylphs. The earthangel of fire is connected with the salamanders (not the animals but the spirit beings called salamanders), and the angel of the water with undines, nixes, and nymphs.

The nature spirits are guided by the thoughts of the angels. They form the bridge to the subtle area of the crystals, plants, and animals, which in turn imprint the material portion of these creations.

Archangels and Karma

Not only the archangel Michael, who is called the "Guardian of Karma," but also all the archangels have power over karma. They can clear karma through the power of grace.

As already mentioned, one of the archangels' goals is that we awaken and become conscious. One aspect of becoming conscious is breaking through karma and recognizing how we create our life. We can recognize the correlations between our patterns, blocks, expectations, thoughts, feelings, and what we encounter in the outside world. And this isn't just a matter of apparent interrelations. When we work with the angels, they lead us deeper, layer by layer. When we recognize one correlation and change it (what would perception be without change?), we will soon discover a further facet of the same theme. We are meant to consciously recognize our own identity down into the last corner of our being. This includes the shadow aspects, as well as the patterns, modes of behavior, and old pain to which we often cling.

However, this also includes the light aspects—and some people have a hard time accepting their own greatness and abilities. I have also noticed time and again how much more pleasant it is to be inconspicuous and keep a low profile, even when I had the urge to be present in the outside world. Whenever I speak to large groups, I still get excited. When I imagine that I have developed all of my abilities and "go out into the world" with them, I still feel queasy. As Nelson Mandela aptly put it: "It is not our darkness that we fear, but our light."

Becoming conscious means recognizing the correlations and leaving our old bogged-down ruts. One step is necessary. We usually know this—yet it is still difficult for us. This is where the angels have an effect: They dissolve patterns and energetic blocks so that it becomes easier for us—but we have to do it ourselves and take the necessary steps.

When we become conscious, giving up the veil, this also clears karma. Karma means that I create an effect with everything that I do or think. And I must neutralize this effect. We become entangled, yet must continue to develop ourselves.

We encounter evil deeds time and again and we must suffer through whatever we have done to others in order to neutralize them. If we speak badly of our disdained colleague, someone will also speak badly of us. Good deeds are like sweets. They also catch up with us and we experience good things to clear them. We could compare karma with a bank account: We can only close it when there is no more money in the account, when we have neither credit nor debits. Creating a balance of zero in "the bank account of karma" is difficult, if not impossible. On the one hand, we still have much to resolve from previous incarnations—karmic entanglements with other people, unresolved learning assignments, good deeds—on the other hand, we create new karma every day.

As long as we move within the realm of karma, we are magnets for life experiences with which we learn to resolve old imbalances. Yet, if we look at the meaning of karma, we discover that it doesn't mean "paying the consequences" but *learning*. The sense of it isn't "an eye for an eye, a tooth for a tooth." We are meant to recognize the connections and become conscious. When the soul decides to take the path of the earth, it elects learning. It wants to have experiences and gain insights.

This is why, for example, the negative experience of power abuse is not negative for the soul. It is an experience, and when the soul has undergone one aspect in which the individual was the perpetrator, it also wants to become familiar with the role of victim. However, if we recognize and understand this without suffering through the victim role, the experience is also complete for the soul. In this situation karma can be resolved through the gift of grace, without having to "pay the consequences."

When we invite the power of the archangels into our life, we no longer need to work off karma, it's enough to look at them and draw our conclusions. Our share is to recognize and translate this into action, which is also easier with the help of the archangels. This can go so far that we must no longer experience situations ourselves but learn through others. What happens to our best friend or partner is often related to us as well. If we recognize what learning steps and what perceptions are involved in the other person's situation, we can avoid getting into such situations to have this experience. If we see how another person falls over a stone that is in the middle of his path, then we are sensible to search our path for the same stone so that we don't fall over it as well. This saves and suffering.

However, there are people who say that "every type of karma is bad for the soul because it continues to be bound to the world as a result" or "karma must be precisely fulfilled, we must do exactly the right thing so that we don't overshoot the completion of karma."[4] As a result, they create a new type of stress: Be sure not to do too much good but do exactly the right thing. But how should I know what exactly is the right thing? In this model of karma, the love and grace of existence isn't taken into consideration. Here God is the bookkeeper who precisely reckons instead of looking at what is important. In this view of karma, the human being does not have the possibility of deciding whether he will continue his path of learning or not: He is tangled in the ties of karma.

I see this differently, and our experiences with the archangels have confirmed my perspective. Some time ago, the spiritual world told me: "You can decide after each incarnation whether to end this path or return to the earth. But why should you stop? That is like leaving in the middle of an exciting film and missing the happy ending."

Living with Angels: Practical Techniques

Why can't we see the angels if they are standing at our side? The simplest answer would be because they are not made of flesh and blood, because they do not belong to our material world, and because we normally just perceive material things with our eyes. Yet, this answer is not convincing when we hear that one-third of the American population has personally experienced the presence of angels *(Fox and Sheldrake)*. If so many people have had this experience, then why can't I—some people may ask themselves. And this brings us back to the topic of how we can perceive angels, archangels, and other spiritual beings. The next question is: How can I make use of their help?

Perceiving Angels

"Do you remember how simple it once was? We appeared to them and put the words in their heart" says the angel Raphaela to Cassriel in Wim Wender's film *Faraway, So Close!* Then he adds: *"At a time when we were the only voices."* Here we find two direct answers to why we normally cannot perceive angels directly with our physical eyes. When they appear, they put words in our heart. And we must therefore be willing to accept these words in our heart.

However, when our heart is closed because of painful experiences, when we no longer let ourselves be touched, how should the angels then appear to us? And even if they appear, how should we recognize them? If they were to become visible to us in the form of human beings, how should we recognize them as angels? If they were to appear to us as angels with wings or as light, our mind would immediately react with: "You are just imagining this." And even if they succeeded in putting the words in our heart, how should we differentiate them from the many other voices within us? Aren't the voices of our mind too loud? No—with the mind, which is also extremely trained for rational thinking, we could not perceive and understand the presence of the angels. Yet, when we still attempt to do this, the result is often something that we can only argue or shake our heads about.

I read that the seraphim are described in the Bible as beings with six wings: "with two they covered their face, with two they covered their feet, with two they flew." The actual Hebraic word used here for "feet" is *regel*. However, this refers to the entire lower body from the toes to the hips. As a result, some authors conclude that the seraphim not only covered their feet with these two wings but also their genitals because it is forbidden to stand naked before God[7]. So, says *Bandini*, the seraphim are sexual and consequently not energetic light beings[1]. But this is not the proper approach. Not only is it unacceptable because a vision was described in the Bible and therefore an image that should not be seen as the portrayal of a reality, but because it is an illogical conclusion.

In my opinion, the statements and images in the Bible should not be understood literally. They have been put into words originating from another age and describe the experience and individual images and visions of human beings. Consequently, we must also look for the true meaning and explore the intended messages. Perceiving and understanding angels occurs on a level that we can call intuition, deep perception, or mystic experience. Their messages usually do not appear in words because words are the tools of the mind. We receive the message in the space of stillness and decode it by immersing ourselves in its vibration and energy, coming into harmony with it, or going into resonance. Angels work behind the scenes. They touch us human beings and then our vibration—our mood—changes. Light comes into the pessimistic thoughts, hope is mixed in with dark emotions, and a feeling of "not being alone" suddenly appears in times of affliction and despair. When we can hear these quiet voices, we can also recognize the angels in them. Yet, such changes are difficult for the logical mind to accept. So I will now describe a few exercises that we can use to train our perception of angels and other subtle vibrations.

Training Our Perception

In order to perceive subtle vibrations, we must place ourselves in an inner state of still attentiveness. In the beginning, this is easier when there is also silence in the space around us and we always practice at the same time and place. There are a great variety of exercises. But they all have the same goal: Achieving a relaxed state by turning down the mind and turning up the inner voice of wisdom or the angels—or whatever inner voice you may want to hear. The first step is to hear the inner voices. To do this, we must dig a path through the many loud thoughts. The second step is to differentiate the inner voices since the voices of fear and expectation, the voices of our childhood, or the warning teachers are mixed in with the voices of wisdom, the higher self, and the angels.

Preparation

Set up a place where you can retreat without being disturbed. Somewhere out in nature is also quite suitable for this purpose. Sit down or lay down comfortably (but be aware that you will more quickly slip into unconsciousness and fail to profit from what you are doing when you lay down). Then invite an angel to strengthen and train your perceptive abilities. Focus your attention inside yourself. Sense inside your body and perceive what areas are tense and which are free and relaxed. Go through your body step by step, from the head to the feet (or the other way around) and allow all the areas that are still tense to relax. If this is difficult for you, then tighten the tensed areas even more until they are almost cramped—and then let go. This is like making a fist and then holding it even tighter—and then letting go.

After you have relaxed your body, direct your attention to your thoughts. Just observe them for a while—and you will be amazed when you start to see how your thoughts bubble up without stopping. The quieter you become, the louder your thoughts will appear to be. Just observe them but don't follow the thoughts. Let them pass by like clouds. At the beginning, you will be caught up in the thoughts. You will see a situation of that day in front of you or remember your shopping spree. Then you will think about what you still have to do today and what you should not forget to do tomorrow—your thoughts have once again become active. This is normal. As soon as you notice this, smile about it and observe the next thoughts that come. In no case should you be annoyed when you stop observing and start actively thinking again. Otherwise, you will get caught up in your annoyance. "It is as it is."

After you have observed the thoughts for a while, turn down the volume of the thoughts—just like you would reduce the volume of the radio. Observe where your attention is now directed. While it may have been in your head before, it may now pull you down into your belly or your heart, or some other area of your body. It doesn't always have to be the same place each time. You can also consciously try out several places and compare them. Then immerse yourself in this inner space and observe what is happening there.

When you do this, it is also helpful to clarify your type of perception: Do you tend to be visual, meaning that you easily see inner images? Or do you tend to be kinesthetic so that you quickly feel things? Or are you auditive (meaning that your inner hearing is the strongest channel)? Most people are kinesthetic, which means that they tend to feel things instead of seeing pictures or hearing voices.

Try this exercise. Close your eyes and imagine: "You are laying in a meadow. You feel the ground beneath your back and the grass that touches your arms and legs. You see the blue sky. When you turn your head to the side, countless varieties of flowers are blooming. The birds are singing. You hear the quiet rustling of the wind in the leaves and perhaps a brook in the distance. The air is filled with the pleasant fragrance of blossoms."

What was easiest for you? You can train your inner senses. Frequently going on inner journeys, doing visualizations, and following imaginary voyages will develop your inner senses. When doing this, it is important to appeal to all the senses: inner images, sounds, feelings, and smells. Whenever you do this exercise, invite an angel to help you.

Meditation and inner journeys can greatly train the perceptive abilities. Yet, as we have said, there is a point when you must differentiate which voice comes from your innermost self, from all of your experiences, from your fears and expectations, and which voice or vibration comes from your inner wisdom, the higher self, your angel or other spiritual helpers. Once you can differentiate between these, there is an additional step: From which level is the voice of the spiritual world coming? There is the astral level, the level of the angels, the ascended masters, the archangels, and countless other beings who can make contact with us. But not all messages are correct or supportive.

In order to train your intuition and perception, you must be able to check whether they are correct. To do this, the best practice areas are found in everyday life: When you buy fruit and vegetables, you can ask which produce tastes good and directly check the answer. You can attune yourself to whether you have mail in the mailbox or who is on the other end when the telephone rings. When you look for an article at the department store or a telephone booth or gas station in a unknown city, follow your inner voice. You will soon notice whether you follow the right voice. When you look for the right path, attune yourself to it. If you suddenly think of someone, call him and ask whether he was thinking about you. How will the weather be tomorrow? Which street or highway will bring you most quickly to your goal?

Train yourself and don't be discouraged if things don't work right away. Practice makes perfect. All individuals bring these abilities with them, just like we all bring the ability of thinking with us. The one person may have an easy time with it, but it may be more difficult for the next. Yet, each of us can train these abilities.

It is also helpful for a group to mutually attune itself to an energy and then describe it. When we do this, we can discover concurrence and open our eyes for areas that we don't usually perceive. Invite an energy or an angel and let its energy flow through your body and your aura. Then describe what you have perceived. This is easier when we apply the LightBeings Essences or spray them around the room. The energy in them is already more material and therefore more easily perceived. In the books on the essences, you will find a description that you can compare to your own perceptions. You can also do the same with gemstones.

Each description and inner perception is individual. Some are closer to the truth, and others are strongly mixed with our own wishful thinking. But don't accept other people's statements as the ultimate truth—comparing the statements in this book with your own perceptions is also a worthwhile approach. In this way, you can increasingly develop your own abilities and powers of discernment.

Creating a Partnership

Asking the Angels

No matter whether you perceive the angels and archangels, they are at your side and waiting for you to invite them. They want to support each human being on his or her path. However, they are not permitted to do this as long as the person does not invite them or request that they do this. Free will is the highest principle and all spiritual beings must respect it. So invite the angels and ask them for support and guidance. You can ask the angels for help in any situation. Angels inspire us and open our eyes to the various possibilities. They arrange encounters and coincidences.

How can we ask something of the angels? Just like we would ask a friend. Just formulate the wish or request silently or loudly. Or you can make a ritual to the angels. Both approaches work. The angel doesn't need the ritual, but it helps *us*. When we direct our attention to our wish, to the situation, we attune ourselves. We put ourselves into a supportive inner state, open ourselves for the vibrations and the encounter. We also intensify our strength, our perception, and our consciousness. And remember that rituals have been celebrated for centuries. This has given them a power of their own, and you can join in this power potential. A ritual works best when you enjoy it and like it because it is meant for you.

Hand over

As described above, archangels serve our awakening. This is why they want us to consciously perceive things. When we consciously learn our steps, then we no longer have to suffer through and experience the old things. I received the technique of hand over from the archangels: Whenever you realize what is blocking you, why you make things so difficult for yourself, which old pattern has struck again, what kinds of resistance you have, that you are stuck in your feelings: surrender to the archangel. Then you will let go and your blocked energies will flow once again. Look at the old problem one more time, feel your way into it. Thank the old problem for serving you and place it in the hands of the archangels.

I work with the image of seeing the difficulty, the feeling, or the situation as a little package that I place in the hands of the archangels. In the same way that you can hand over a veil that you no longer like, you can give everything to the archangels. Things will change! Even if it takes time, the best thing will happen. Sometimes it won't change in the way that you desire it to, because what you expected was not the best.

Whenever I have handed over something to the archangel, the result was that something happened. I often have experienced that I became conscious of my next step. If, for example, the matter was clarifying a situation, I quickly felt what I had to do after placing it in their hands. Sometimes I passed on this step as well because I didn't feel like doing it. I asked the archangels to clarify things even more for me. And then there was often a big bang. The clarification I had dodged became a conflict—and cleared itself up.

We can place everything into the hands of the archangels: wishes, hopes, dreams, difficulties, uncertainties, half-baked things, old matters, pain, healing—everything. They will do their part and what we must do, will become clear to us.

Some people have problems with handing over things: "Things just can't work this easily." "But I have to at least sit down and clarify things before I can hand them over or make a request," "We aren't allowed to bother angels with such unclear stuff, with such profane things" is what I often hear. This is also a way of dodging the matter.

Angels want us to awaken and live fulfilled lives, which is why they support us in every situation. Perhaps it isn't always the archangel Raphael, even when you ask him or put your veil in his hands. Perhaps he will delegate the matter to the "appropriate" angel. Yet, this isn't your problem. Your job is to ask and hand over the matter. Observe what happens when you do this.

Handing over things is also difficult because we aren't used to doing it. Since most of us have grown up without the image of the helping angels, we have learned to do everything on our own. And so I often do not realize how many different things I could hand over to them.

Some time ago, one of the seminars that I lead was canceled because of a lack of participants. I considered this a gift from heaven because I had once again loaded myself down with too many things and no longer had any free time. However, at the same time the old absurd fear welled up that people were no longer interested in my seminars and the essences and everything would collapse. This fear breathed down my neck for quite a while before I remembered to hand it over. Then the fear was gone in a second and I once again felt completely well.

Whenever there are difficulties, whenever you feel unwell, whenever you have unpleasant feelings or oppressive thoughts, train yourself to take an exact look at the situation. Perceive what is happening and then hand it over to the angels with the request that they clear it up for you.

Placing Angels at Our Side— Further Techniques

- A wonderful technique is to lay yourself in the arms of an angel or archangel. Imagine or feel how you lay in their arms and allow yourself to sink into them. This is especially healing in crisis situations.
- Whenever you think of it or when you need to, imagine how an angel walks at your side and accompanies you. Perhaps you can also perceive what he says.
- In healing work, I can ask an angel or archangel to guide me and let his power work through me. I can call on him in any therapy and ask that he facilitates the client's work or heals him or her. And I can ask the angel to accompany and protect the client for a while longer when this is in harmony with the divine plan and corresponds with the client's will. In this way, I can also send healing angels to people in different places and ask them to help the people. They do this when the other human being agrees and help is allowed within the framework of the divine order.
- In the same way, I can ask the angels for guidance and inspiration in any other activity—no matter whether I am teach-

ing, writing, driving the car, heading a company, or taking care of my children. This gives us access to higher consciousness and knowledge.

- I can also place angels at the sides of other people. I have already done this often during conversations or telephone calls when the other person wasn't doing very well. I visualize that an angel is standing next to them, hugging them, and giving them energy and love. It is wonderful to see how the other person's mood changes without doing anything yourself. We can also send guardian angels along with children when they go to school, when the partner drives to work, or to accompany people who are in difficult situations. *We are naturally only permitted to do this in harmony with the divine plan and the other person's free will.* Otherwise, the intervention will reflect back on us. This is why I always add this thought to my request of the angels: "*This only should happen if the other person's higher consciousness agrees and it is included in the divine plan.*"

Cleansing, Harmonizing, and Charging Rooms

I can ask angels to clear rooms and fill them with their energy. This is particularly effective in negatively charged rooms and places. Here as well, I ask for "*harmony with the divine plan and the best for all participants.*"

Angel Conference

The angel conference is a special inner ritual. You can call for this conference at any time when you need direction or clarity. Then go to your place of meditation and your inner space. Imagine how all the angels and helpers who can support you in the situation are sitting at the table there. Present your request or describe the situation. Then listen to what the individual helpers have to say and what advice they can give you. The helpers will also give you gifts that will help you take the next step. Accept these gifts. In conclusion, ask them for further support and thank the spiritual beings.

Ask Anything

We are allowed to call on angels at any time and in all situations. A person doesn't have to be "holy" or "worthy" to do this. We also don't have to be at the end of our possibilities and powers. Life becomes easier when we include the angels from the start and not just when we are stuck. Every situation, every experience, even when it appears very banal to us, serves the path of awakening consciousness. The more we learn to include help from the spiritual world in our everyday life and use it in common matters, the stronger our connection will be and the clearer our perception. And we learn to differentiate between when we can receive gifts and when we must do something ourselves—because the angels don't just take care of everything.

There is a difference in the help of the angels and the archangels, as already explained above. Angels are powers who always stand at our side for everything. They also fulfill our wishes. Archangels serve the process of becoming conscious, the recognition of the true nature within us. When you have wishes, you can feel whether these are more a task for the angels or for the archangels. You actually cannot do anything wrong since angels are not public officials who first examine their competency and then ignore the course of events. The right angels or helpers will do their work, even if you ask "the wrong ones" or just make a general request. But since this is a matter of awakening and recognition, our perception and sensing serve us in becoming more conscious.

You can ask angels to help you find a parking spot, to keep the street free of traffic when you drive on the freeway, to help you find the right route and arrive on time, to help you find the right partner, to help you have a wonderful vacation, and that a new place to live will turn up in accordance with your wishes. And you should remember to add: "may this or something better occur."

Some people believe that they are not allowed to ask angels and archangels for money or material things. Yet, the material world is the world in which we live. Material things are the treasures of the material world. It is an expression of self-love when we allow ourselves to live in beauty, prosperity, and wealth. When we love ourselves, we can take and give. And we recognize that the universe is abundant and this abundance is also part of our existence. Material abundance is an expression of universal abundance. Next to relationships, money and wealth is our greatest learning field. Many people get stuck here in self-judgment, old patterns, guilt feelings, inferiority complexes, and the concept of not being worthy or not being permitted to have things.

However, we may not necessarily receive the millions that we desire from the angels. Not because we aren't allowed to have them, but because we block ourselves unconsciously and do not recognize it. Or because the path without the millions is better for us. The process of becoming conscious is involved here. People often do not allow themselves to ask or demand. They practice modesty and tell themselves that they actually don't need anything and already have everything. When they look more deeply into themselves, the wishes become visible. The unfulfilled wishes that we do not see are also part of the shadow that darkens the light of consciousness. Everything that we ask the angels for becomes a learning step and serves our awakening. The angels make sure of this. For example, if we ask for money and receive it, this will be connected with a learning step.

Angelic Partners

Seraphim

While the archangels and angels are more intensively in contact with human beings, the cherubim and seraphim tend to be associated with the divine realms. It is written in the Bible that they stand at the throne of God, which means that they are the closest to God—to the origin.

Seraphim means "inflamer" or "igniter." The Hebraic root of the word is *saraph* and means burning, consuming, or glowing. They are the angels of light, of love, and of the divine fire. In the Bible, they carry a glowing coal with which they touch Isaiah's lips so that he is cleansed *(Isaiah 6)*. Through this burning heat, he is immediately freed of all blame.

In contrast to the cherubim, of whom only rustling and thunder can be heard, constant songs of praise sound from the seraphim. This is also described in *Revelations 4.8*. If we resonate with their energy, we will be flooded with overflowing joy, love, and light. It is the ecstasy of the Creation, which glows in complete joy and sings a song of praise in overflowing gratitude. Its sound lets the entire Creation vibrate and we can also be caught up in it, as if in the gentle radiance of ebullience and love. It almost appears as if we ourselves turn into light. In this power, it is difficult to adjust to the body again.

The seraphim are described in the Bible as beings with six wings: with two they cover their face, two wings cover their feet, and with the other two they fly.

Cherubim

The cherubim are called the guardians of the Garden of Eden in the Bible. With flaming, flashing swords they guard the path to the Tree of Life *(Genesis 3.24)*. They prevent people who are not ready from entering Paradise, the unity. But, as a result, they are also the link to the unity.

In other places in the Bible, the cherubim are also described as the guardians of the divine and the holy places. They are present as statues above the Ark of the Covenant *(Exodus 25.18)* and form the space in which Moses can encounter God. They protect the room in which the Ark is kept *(1 Kings 8.6)*. Ezekiel sees them in his visions and describes them as beings with four wings and four faces: one ox, one lion, one eagle, and one human face. This means that they bear the symbols of the four elements. When the cherubim move, their wings rustle like great waters, in a loud roar. When they stand still, it sounds like thunder *(Ezekiel 1.10)*.

The cherubim appear to Ezekiel as enormous, powerful, and mighty beings. It is difficult to come in contact with them. And when we attune ourselves to their energy, they are foreign, somehow not related to us, and impersonal. They appear in an abundance that is not comprehensible. Their name means "guardian of insight" or "outpouring of knowledge."

They are very close to the divine force and have the ability of receiving the direct vibration of God and passing it on to others. This makes them an important interface between the divine impulses and the beings of materialization. The symbols of the four elements illustrate that they are connected with the elements, perhaps even that they are the first impulse of these elements and of matter.

Elohim

The elohim described here belong to the golden ray. They are the elohim of returning home. There are still other groups of elohim that have different tasks.

Themes
Cleansing of outside energies, companions into the realm of light.

Description of the Energy
The elohim of the golden ray are called "the angels of returning home." Their power is light, loving, and connecting.

General Tasks
The elohim of the golden ray are the companions of souls as they leave the body and change over into the realm of light. As a result, the elohim also clear places, rooms, and other beings when the souls or other energies and entities "get stuck" there. They often work together with the elohim of the silver ray of grace, which pardons and clears karma.

Tasks for Human Beings
The elohim also support human beings in freeing themselves from outside energies and forces that do not belong to them. These are not necessarily just earthbound souls (see explanation under "About this Theme." They also free us from thought forms, emotions, and karmic entanglements that we can let go of. The elohim sometimes work together with the Archangel Michael. Together with human beings, they can bring lost and earthbound souls into the realm of light.

About this Theme
Souls normally go into the light when they leave the earthly body after death. The angels of returning home accompany

them on this path. However, some souls do not choose this path and stay on the earth instead.

These are called the earthbound or lost souls. They so intensely concentrate on the earth and life on earth that they no longer perceive the levels of light or are afraid of them. Perhaps you have seen the movie *Ghost*. This topic is taken up and visually depicted in the film: After Sam has left his body, at first he doesn't comprehend that he has died. When a ray of light appears that draws him, he decides to stay with his girlfriend and his dead body—and the ray of light disappears again.

Sam has therefore lost the opportunity of returning to the realm of light. Only at the end, when he has completed his task, does the ray of light appear again and Sam's soul leaves the earth. This film shows that some souls still want to take care of a task before they are willing to leave the earth. Some do not want to leave a beloved person or want to stand by someone (sometimes they are also held here by the partner or someone else who loves them).

When death occurs so suddenly that the person did not reckon with it—such as in an accident, a disaster, or a natural catastrophe—some souls are in a state of shock. They do not notice and comprehend that their bodies no longer exist (as happened to Sam at first in the film). They believe that they are still alive. Certain souls are filled with anger, hatred, and despair (especially when they have been killed or fall in a war), and want revenge or redress. These intense feelings then prevent them from letting go and turning to the realm of light.

Other souls have lived against their inner concept of "good" and believe that they are "evil" or have done something bad. These souls have guilt feelings and believe they have lost the right to return to the light. This is why they do not see the ray of grace that guides every soul into the realm of light, no matter how the person has lived his or her life. Or they do not trust it.

The spiritual beings of love do not judge. Everything that we do in life serves our development. We have experiences between the poles of good and evil, and we can or must use these experiences for the development of the soul. Some people learn their lessons through the "evil pole," others learn them through suffering, and others through joy and happiness.

Earthbound souls usually cannot find the bridge into the realm of light on their own. They often just see people and other earthbound energies since they still identify with human existence. They cannot perceive the powers of light and the angels.

Yet, we human beings can create the connection between these souls and the elohim. Almost all religions either had or still have rituals in order to help these lost souls return home.

When people have the feeling of wanting to do something in this area, they should turn to an individual who is experienced and trained to do this. The dissolving of symbioses in particular should only be carried out by people who have the therapeutic training to also accompany the people involved in the situation.

Possession

Most earthbound souls stay in places or rooms, frequently those where their death took place. Some connect with the energy field of a human being. This is then called possession.

As also described under the Archangel Michael, these souls or outside energies can only attach themselves where there is a resonance surface, a similar vibration, or a related theme. And the human being must agree to let this happen. So this "possession" is not like occupying an empty house—the house has no opportunity for deciding whether it wants to be taken or not. Instead, it is much more like codependency, which is why I will also use the word "symbiosis" in the following instead of "possession." This term expresses that the human being is not a defenseless victim who has been attacked. Both parties, the "possessed person" and the "earthbound soul," profit from this state. This is just like the symbiosis in the plant realm, where both the plant and the parasite have advantages, even if the intruder harms the plant.

This consent is usually given unconsciously. The waking consciousness knows nothing of it. Consequently, many people think it is implausible and incomprehensible to think that they have agreed to the possession. They cannot imagine why they would give an outside, unpleasant, and energy-robbing being— a strange soul—the permission to interfere. What do the two parties get from each other?

The earthbound soul receives energy, strength, and the feeling of once again having a body and being alive. It can intervene in the life and will of the person, influencing his feelings, moods, and actions. This can even lead to a split personality. Seen from the outside, this person now has two faces that act and react in completely different ways. Or the individual may behave in a way that is completely different from his normal behavior.

The person also feels like he is no longer completely himself. In some situations, he will react in ways that would otherwise be foreign to him. He will wonder why he behaves in this way, yet cannot change. Sometimes he may feel very tired or as if he no longer has contact with his body.

The human being wants to learn a certain theme. As a result, he opens the door for this soul who can help him with this theme or make certain things clear to him for once. These themes may be: perceiving that he feels himself to be a helpless victim; developing his strength; recognizing that he doesn't live completely in his body and learning to completely fill it out; dealing with emotions; resolving conflicts with deceased persons; resolving themes like power, envy, greed, or addiction. Every unresolved theme can attract a soul that also continues to be involved with this issue.

Ultimately, earthbound souls seek deliverance. And this is where the elohim offer their help. They form a bridge upon which the soul can return back to the realm of light. Another individual or therapist can serve as the mediator here.

When a symbiosis is dissolved, it is important to encounter the soul in love and enable it to return to the realm of light. It doesn't help to just throw the soul out of the connection with a human being because it will immediately look for the next symbiosis partner or return to the same one after a while.

Clearing Our Own Resonance Surface

People who "remove" such outside energies often have the experience that they cannot truly be removed when the respective person has not yet resolved the theme. There are effective methods for ending the symbiosis and sending the soul into the light, even if the person knows nothing of this work. However, if the affected person has not yet learned his lesson, his energy system will attract other earthbound souls who have the same pattern.

An Experience

Some time ago, I went to visit an institute for problem children. I could perceive that there were many earthbound souls hanging around there. So I asked the elohim to form their bridge and invited all the souls who were ready to go to use this bridge. However, not all of them were willing and the room remained filled with these souls. I recognized that, on the one hand, they served the children; on the other hand, through the processes and steps taken by the children, the souls could also resolve part of their own past and their own lives. They participated in experiences that served them. The souls also didn't form a symbiosis with the children but just remained in the rooms.

When we left the house, I felt a deep sadness within me. I felt like crying—which astonished me because I had felt very good beforehand. At first, I believed this was related to the impressions there and my consternation about this hard path of life. But when I looked at the deeper aspects, I felt that a soul had come along with me and entered my energy system. Since I had a great deal to take care of that day, I didn't do anything about it at first. I asked the elohim several times to clear me; when this didn't have the right effect, I called on the Archangel Michael. There was brief relief, but the sadness remained.

When I was still so sad the next day, I knew that *I* had something to learn and had to take a more precise look at things. I was quite familiar with this unfounded sadness from earlier in my life: I had sometimes spent days and weeks in this state without being possessed. Yet, this hadn't occurred in years. In meditation, I called upon the ray of the elohim and my spiritual helpers. Then I made room for the soul. I let myself fall into this sadness and mentally formulated the words that came up. There were vehement accusations against the spiritual world: "You have let us down. First you send us down here and promise that you will accompany us and stand by us. But when we need you, you abandon us. Traitors! I can't trust you anymore!"

Once the anger had been vented, tears came to my eyes and the longing returned: "I want to go back home, I want to go back into the light. Please take me with you. I want to return." And I noticed how I felt lighter and something was resolved within me. The sadness had disappeared, the soul had gone into the light, and I was once again as joyful as before the visit to the children's institution. Until this soul had expressed its pain and therefore let go of it, it hadn't been prepared to go into the light.

And I also had to look once again at my old pattern. I had also experienced life on earth as a being who had been kicked out; within me was also the experience of having been left alone. Although, as a result of reincarnation sessions, I had seen that I had personally chosen this learning experience and had healed a great deal, remnants of this feeling still existed within me. I had not yet accepted the suffering involved in the path of duality. In addition, I still was hurt by the reality of how people suffer and souls burden themselves with a difficult path. I had not completely reconciled myself with the learning opportunities of duality that people choose for themselves.

After I had seen this, something healed within me. The outside soul had taken part of my pain along with it into the light. I felt myself to be in peace and love with the path. And I was willing to get involved more deeply in life, to live my abilities, my joy, and my easiness even more intensely. It had been time to take this step, but I had once again tried to dodge it and didn't even see it at first.

In addition, I had the experience with this soul exactly at the time when I wanted to write this chapter. I thanked the soul for its help. A few days later, I once again went on an inner journey with my friend Shantidevi—and the same theme came up again: the pain of being separated, of being left in the lurch by the spiritual world, of not truly becoming reconciled with the duality. However, I now could finally embrace the dark pole.

There are places where earthbound souls gather on a large scale: areas where there have been wars, where there are orphanages, prisons, psychiatric institutions, and sites of disasters where many people have suddenly died violent deaths, cemeteries, the crypts of churches, as well as gambling casinos.

When I once visited a gambling casino, I perceived how "gambler souls" were waiting to find a person through whom they could once again live out their passion for gambling. Some people gamble as if they were possessed, bet all of their money and more against their better judgment, and cannot stop gambling.

Other people have stable psyches and can place their bets in a well-considered and concentrated manner. They are not receptive for such souls. None of these souls tried to join me because I don't have a passion for gambling. Since it isn't my learning theme, I don't provide a resonance surface for it.

If someone has the feeling of living in a symbiosis with an outside soul, it is important for an experienced therapist to participate in the healing. The therapist should not only know how to deal with these types of symbioses but also have enough experience in dealing with human learning steps and blind spots. The afflicted person often does not want to see the theme behind the symbiosis because he is not yet able to cope with it or doesn't know how to resolve it.

Meditation

Invite the ray of the elohim to surround you and envelop you. Allow it to permeate your aura and also fill up your body, down into each individual cell. Ask the elohim to dissolve everything that no longer serves you, that doesn't belong to you, and that prevents you from living who you actually are. Ask them to dissolve everything that can now be resolved and, if it is important for you, to let you become aware of it now or later. Ask them to transform the oppressive thought patterns, the obstructive modes of behavior, or the feelings that haven't been healed yet so that they are available to you as strength.

The Archangels

If we classify the archangels according to their vibrations, Metatron is the highest archangel. Sometimes he is no longer considered one of the archangels. Metatron stands on the threshold between form and non-form. Jophiel and Zadkiel are on the next level. Both create a connection between the higher and lower areas and can let energies and impulses ascend and descend. The archangels on the third level are those who sustain and elucidate the divine aspects or principles: Michael, Raphael, Gabriel, Chamuel, Haniel, and Uriel.

Uriel

In Judaism, Uriel is one of the oldest angels in the immediate vicinity of God. He is considered the regent of the star world and guardian of its laws[14].

Themes
Creative force, initiative, structure, decisiveness, peace, harmony, rapport between the divine plan and material structure, manifestation, transformation, bringing the divine vibration into the material world.

Description of the Energy
Uriel is the most earthly and solid of the archangels. He is most intensely connected with the earth. On the bridge between the divine and the earthly, he forms the bridgehead to the material world. His energy is powerful, strengthening, stabilizing, structure-giving, organizing, energizing, and yet, calm. It helps in setting us in motion and directing our strength at a goal.

As its main color, the Uriel energy is associated with garnet and ruby red. His name means: God's fire, God's light, flame of the sun, the light that comes from God.

General Tasks
Uriel is the archangel of order, structure, materialization, and crystallization. He holds the key to the material world. He anchors the powers of light, the divine, and consciousness in matter. The divine plan is translated into matter and connected with consciousness. Uriel reigns over the creation of material structures in order to form beings according to the divine plan, to let situations and cornerstones arise and connect them with consciousness. The original energy is transformed down through the various levels and ultimately passed on to the powers of the materialization ray. This is how matter is formed and situations are created.

But Uriel can also bring structures and processes of development that deviate from the intended plan back into the cosmic order. As a result, he is the guardian of the divine order in all material structures. The effect of his energy on the earth is to provide structure; for example, on the earth's grid network and in the restoration and reconstruction after destruction and catastrophes.

Tasks for Human Beings

As the guardian of order and matter, Uriel teaches us to master the material world. He helps human beings reconnect with the divine order and live in harmony with it. He brings us into the here and now, carries consciousness into the ordinary world, and helps us live our spirituality in everyday life.

Since money is also an expression of the divine force in the material world, he shows us how matter, wealth, and spirituality can be brought into harmony. But he also helps people who have become too entangled in matter and too attached to money and their physical nature. He opens the way for them to once again connect with their divine aspect and the meaning of their life.

Uriel is the guardian of the physical body and harmonizes the body, mind, and soul. He strengthens the ability to listen to the wisdom of the body, which results in strengthening the structures and connection between the subtle and physical bodies. Consequently, he also has a supportive effect in healing activities.

Uriel shows us all the areas in which the material reality does not correspond with the divine plan or ideal. Especially in the areas of the home, the body, relationships, taking our place in the world, and money—the most popular spiritual learning themes—the unfulfilled wishes appear. This dissatisfaction makes us aware that the reality does not correspond with the ideal for which we strive.

By once again bringing material reality into harmony with the intended ideal state, he helps when we want to create an ideal body. Where and why the body has left the ideal order and how it can achieve this once again becomes clear. In comparison to Raphael, who heals through love, Uriel brings us back into the structure. This can also cause healing to occur.

Uriel is also described as the archangel for peace and devotion. He resolves the tension between the planned and the actual state. He creates the peace between what exists and our visions or human expectations.

As the guardian of matter, his energy can also be used by scientists to illuminate the laws of matter.

About This Theme

The physical body is formed through earthly matter and through subtle energy. It expresses the interaction between food, other substances that we absorb (for example, environmental toxins, medications), the subtle cosmic and earthly energies, our inner patterns, and spiritual learning steps. When, for example, someone lives with the thought: "If I just look at a piece of cake I get fat," he usually has the tendency of quickly gain weight. The opposite occurs for people who say: "I can eat what I want and stay slender."

Spiritual learning steps and blocks in the subtle energy field are also reflected in the body if we don't recognize and resolve them beforehand. It is now widely known that there is a correlation between our illness and our learning steps. Since Uriel helps us to adjust the physical body to the ideal image, his energy makes us aware of these correlations and helps resolve them. We experience an increased willingness to open up to the earth and life here. It becomes easier to grow roots, which means that the challenges of life are also mastered more easily. Life becomes more cheerful.

Some spiritual people have a shortage of money. They believe—whether consciously or unconsciously—that success, wealth, status, prestige, and money cannot be combined with a spiritual life. This attitude has also been reinforced in past centuries and within many traditions. The Bible says: "It is easier for a camel to go through the eye of a needle than for a rich man to enter the kingdom of God." *(Luke 18.25)* And on our paths in previous lives, we have probably had the experience that money, possessions, and power imprisoned us. While we enjoyed the luxury, our connection with the divine force withered. At the end of life, we drew the conclusion that "money has ruined me, I will never again get involved with the joys of the material world."

But avoiding something doesn't mean that we have learned this lesson. For many people—and especially when they were born in the Western world—it's time to recognize that money and wealth are an expression of divine abundance. It's time to learn how they can be used in a positive way that supports us and other people. A hammer is only useful when we pick it up. "It is more blessed to give than to receive"—but what can an empty fountain give?

Experiences

The first reaction that I had to the Uriel energy was a leaden tiredness. Once again, vehement resistance against my own strength raged within me. I no longer wanted to be rooted in the earthly realm and grow. During this time, we searched for a larger building for the company—and the Uriel Essence allowed me to become conscious of my resistance and constricting beliefs about houses, money, and growth. I recognized what caused me to block my strength and once again became aware of the images of helplessness that I had assumed from my parents.

The same thing was repeated a bit later with regard to bringing the LightBeings Master Essences to the USA from Germany. Through the application of the Uriel Essence, I was ultimately able to dissolve blocks and a pleasant, easy path opened up. Strength, initiative, and self-assurance flowed through me. I began to structure the course of my day, to plan things, and straighten up the overflowing desk, the old files, and cabinets. I once again paid more attention to the needs of my body and strengthened it through sports, cleansing methods, and cold baths in order to make it more powerful, healthy, and stable.

Other people have told us about similar reactions. They regained their vigor and felt awake and lively. They could hardly sleep at night after working with the Uriel energy or essence during the evening. They understood their own situation and perspective, as well as sharpening their eyes for what is important in life. People have recognized their blocks and turned their visions into reality. They have courageously and purposefully created order and tackled the tasks ahead of them. At the same time, they felt so serene that they did not take any premature actions.

People who have read a great deal, who have overloaded themselves with theoretical knowledge, report that they put their books aside and began to try out what they had read, putting the knowledge to practice, after working with the Uriel Essence.

Some people who used it were confronted with the issues of money and relationships—the "most popular learning themes." This involved bringing the ideal, the wish, into harmony with the earthly reality. Deviations in both of these areas have a particularly strong effect on human beings.

Good to Use in the Following Situations
• When you feel weak and inflexible
• Rigidity in the body
• When the body doesn't correspond to the ideal form
• When you lack the courage to turn your visions into reality
• For manifesting, creating, and materializing
• In phases lacking structure and against chaos
• For success in your profession, at work, in the business realm
• Since it strengthens the powers of the body, the essence can also be used in situations where the body needs additional energy: when you have eaten something heavy or indigestible or in stress situations
Works together with the energies of:
• the Ascended Masters Aeolus, Kamakura, and Serapis Bey
• the complementary Earthangel Earth

Meditation

Become like a seed, a flower seed that rests in the earth. It is surrounded by the warming, nourishing, dark soil that softly nestles against it. The seed slowly absorbs water and nutrients from the soil and begins to activate its vital force. A seed already contains everything, just as everything that you need to develop is already within you. Although it looks inconspicuous and small from the outside, almost like any other seed, it already contains within it the idea of the flower into which it desires to develop. There are already little roots, a small stem, and tiny leaves in the seed.

At the same time, it carries the image of the grown and blossomed plant within it. The tiny plant bears the image of the roots and the leaves; it knows how high the stem can stretch toward the sun, how many blossoms are possible, and which color the flowers will have. The flower is already contained within the seed in its full beauty and greatest development.

However, whether the plant grows into this potential depends upon the plant itself. Just like it is up to you whether you grow into the potential that you have brought with you and fill it out. Does the little plant use its strength to anchor its roots deep within the earth and sprout its stem so high that it remains stable, even if a strong wind blows—or does the stem remain short or grow beyond the optimal length? Does it use its strength to form blossoms and fruit? Does it then produce rich, fertile fruit? The ideal image of what is possible already exists within the seed.

And so the little seed begins to grow, just as you grow. First you burst your seed capsule and push your roots into the earth. The roots anchor you in the nourishing soil and begin to draw nutrients and water into the seed so that the stem can be formed. And then the stem also pushes up through the soil with its first little leaves until it has left the dark earth realm and entered into the brightness of day. You drink in the sunlight and grow. The stem becomes stronger and more and more leaves develop and nourish the entire plant.

And finally, the buds and blossoms form, which will bloom and be fertilized at the right point in time. And perhaps you recognize what plant you have blossomed into. Little fruits with seeds are created through the fertilization. And as the petals fall, the seeds ripen—and once again they bear within them the ideal image of a complete flower. When the seed has ripened and carries enough nutrients within it to supply the new plant that is already planned within it, it leaves the parent plant and falls onto the fertile ground at some point. It rests a while there until the right time has come for it to absorb nutrients and grow.

Feel how you carry the strength of this plant within you, how you can already let all your visions and abilities grow so that they appear in a material form. Feel how this strength flows through your body. Then take a deep breath and be completely present again in the here and now.

Haniel

Themes

Knowledge, recognizing and living your own greatness, living consciously every day, clear perception, seeing through illusions, taking action in a self-evident manner, essence of being, joy, strength, self-confidence, self-assurance, sublimity, serene stillness.

Description of the Energy

Although we get the impression of an intensely powerful, uplifting, royal strength, the energy of Haniel is very gentle. It connects higher consciousness with earthly power. At the same time, it centers and relaxes us.

The main color vibration of Haniel is light blue.

General Tasks

Haniel's energy gives every life the power to lift itself up, to align itself and therefore grow into its own greatness. The original purpose and form is assumed. It strengthens, clarifies, and balances energies.

Tasks for Human Beings

Haniel's energy is like a ray of light, a laser ray in which we can put ourselves. It uplifts us, reminds us of who we really are, which abilities we have, and gives us the courage to live these qualities. It strengthens so that we can walk our path in a straightforward, consistent, and sincere manner. Gnawing self-doubt and feelings of "being unworthy" dissolve and we succeed in accepting the challenges and the surrounding world, as well as opening up to the outside world. People feel the desire to take action and have an effect on the world. We express our truth and act in accordance with it. We recognize that we are also a pillar of light, with aspects of consciousness and abilities on many levels. We are a self-evident form of existence and experience a heart-centered resting within ourselves.

But we not only come to know ourselves. Haniel helps us to see through illusions. We can ultimately also succeed in seeing through the illusion of separation, of duality, of so-called reality—the Indians call it *maya*.

With Haniel's strength, we human beings recognize that developing and showing our potential is also part of living a fulfilled life. If we hide ourselves and make ourselves smaller than we actually are, we will seldom experience what effects we can have on the world. Haniel dissolves degrading thought and behavior patterns. When we reconnect with our light, these patterns vanish on their own like soap bubbles. The thought forms behind illness and complaints can also be recognized and dissolved in this manner. Haniel makes us aware of where we stand, what the next step is, and gives us the courage to take this step.

About This Theme

Accepting our own greatness and living it does not mean boasting, arrogance, or feeling superior to others but recognizing and naturally living our abilities and qualities. This involves valuing ourselves. Arrogance and feelings of superiority lead to separating ourselves from others. Then we put ourselves on a pedestal and create a distance to other people. We ultimately become lonely and no longer let anything move us. Sometimes the fear of our own arrogance prevents us from accepting our strength.

Yet, if we remain in our heart, in a loving relationship to our fellow human beings, we will not fall into presumption and arrogance. We will let ourselves be moved and put ourselves on the same level as others, even if they think we are ahead or better, and even if they place us on a pedestal.

If we live our own vastness, our own light, other people also become encouraged to live their light. Developing and living our own abilities does not have to be strenuous and difficult. When we naturally live our talents and have trust in ourselves, we will succeed in much more than we believe we can.

However, we sometimes consider the acquired self-image to be authentic and forget our true being: We have fallen in the mud and believe that the dirt sticking to us is part of our actual appearance. That others also see us like this intensifies this impression. Yet, washing would suffice to reveal our true appearance. But why should we wash when we believe that this muddy appearance corresponds to our own being?

Haniel is a teacher of the theme of illusions and expectations. He not only makes us aware of our concealed expectations, but also shows us which expectations are justified and which are inappropriate. It's quite clear that we can't expect an orange to bring light into a dark room. However, some expectations that we have of our partner, other people, situations, or ourselves are just as inappropriate. But we don't notice it. Only when we have been disappointed by our expectations time and again are we perhaps willing to examine them to see if they are appropriate.

Experiences

When I worked with the Haniel Essence, I was able to recognize my patterns and inner feelings much more faster. For example, that I didn't allow myself any breaks while working, that I, despite feeling worn out, first attended to the needs of our customers. I easily recognized the patterns reflected by others.

I also learned to use the image of a pillar of light, as described in the meditation. When I had difficulties or was burdened by old ideas, I visualized the pillar of light in which I could stand in my greatness and perfect being.

Other people also reported that they had confrontations at their working situation and the aspects of equality during the time with Haniel. Old patterns and mistakes became obvious. Decisions became easier. They felt caressed and protected by the energy. They became more single pointed and felt stronger.

Use in the Following Situations
- To dissolve blocks of using abilities
- Against self-doubt, when you don't believe yourself being capable of anything
- In decision-making situations
- When you deny your own truth out of fear or hopelessness.
- In situations of feeling bent and hopeless because of worry
- For clear perception, to strengthen your third eye
- The essence can also strengthen flowers, plants, and animals

Works together with the energies of:
- the Ascended Masters Sanat Kumara, Maha Chohan, Orion, Helion, and Hilarion
- the complementary Earthangel Tree

Meditation

Direct your attention to your body. Which areas are free and relaxed? Which areas are tense? While you go through your entire body, allow yourself to relax and loosen up the areas that are tense. Just like ice melts in the sunshine, your body can also become more relaxed. And then invite the energy of Haniel. It is like a powerful pillar of light that appears next to you. But you may also perceive it differently, in your own way. Observe how large this pillar of light or the energy is, how much space it fills up. How high does it extend up into the sky? How is it connected with the earth? Feel the power and the gentleness that radiates from it.

This pillar of light, this energy form is a mirror of your own greatness, your own light. And while you perceive this pillar of light, you can now also see how you perceive yourself. How large do you appear to yourself? How bright and filled with light are you? Where do your oppressive convictions cling to you like dark shadows?

Now enter the energy of Haniel with complete consciousness and become this light, this power. The oppressive convictions and thought patterns are transformed into light-filled strengths. Perceive how your inner light develops, blossoms like a flower, and stands in its full dimensions. Allow yourself to be enveloped by the love of Haniel and all of your blocks and resistance against your own greatness melt away like frozen ice. Now the previously constricted energy can become free and fill you so that it becomes easier for you to stand up in your full size and let your light shine.

Chamuel

(Also called Chamael, Camael, or Khameal)

Themes

Harmony, easiness, exhilaration, higher vibrations, creativity, inspiration, beauty, relationships, partnership, empathy.

Description of the Energy

The energy of Chamuel is cheerful, light, gentle, exalting, lovingly enveloping, soft, supportive, and at the same time powerful. Some people feel it to be like a hearty hug. It raises the vibrations, as if the wings of the angels would carry us.

The name means "God is my destination" or "He who seeks God."

The corresponding color is pink to salmon-orange.

General Tasks

Chamuel manifests the aspects of the divine beauty in matter. He is responsible for the relationship between everything that has been created. With the power of love, he connects and separates, creates harmony, and increases the vibrational frequency. As a result, he orients everything that has been created toward perfection, toward the highest destiny, toward God. This is also shown by his name: God is my destination. He is also called the angel of evolution, of development.

Tasks for Human Beings

Through the power of love, Chamuel has the ability to lead us out of every kind of exaggerated attachment. Just like a hot-air balloon rises, he lifts people out of emotional entanglements, out of fears, worries, and afflictions. Hope and feelings of well-being replace the heaviness. We feel a sense of security, of being loved, and become cheerful once again. We can enjoy the game of life.

Chamuel also increases the vibration in places or in rooms and brings deep peace and trust. He teaches us to let ourselves be supported by life and the divine energy.

But before a balloon can rise in the air, the ballast must be thrown overboard. And so we become conscious of what kind of ballast we drag around with us: oppressive attitudes, expectations, and the patterns of behavior to which we cling.

Chamuel also helps us integrate new energies and harmonize the energy system after growth steps and processes of cognition. For the theme of relationships and partnerships, Chamuel is the expert. He clarifies and harmonizes all types of relationships: the relationship with ourselves, with others, with nature, and with God. No matter whether this means the relationship to the beloved, to the partner, to friends, between parents and children, or between business partners, the Chamuel energy reveals the inconsistencies.

He offers his help in all of these situations and shows how we can restore disturbed harmony. He connects people with understanding and empathy, opening our eyes so that we can comprehend the situation and also recognize the divine in the other person. This gives us the courage to reconcile.

Since we can also take a loving look at our own situation and perceive the divine within ourselves, his power also leads to self-love and tolerance for our own weaknesses and mistakes. Through empathy, it is possible for us to recognize ourselves in others and to use this outer mirror in order to recognize, accept, and resolve our own shadow aspects. It becomes easier to look consciously at everything because we no longer judge ourselves and others based on shadow aspects.

Chamuel is also called the angel of charity and tolerance. Since he brings divine beauty to earth, he inspires all of the artistic activities. Through the things that have been created—no matter whether pictures, music, texts, clothing, interior furnishings, or a garden—people are moved, delighted, and their mood improves. His energy is present when we pray, sing, and dance, as well as at soul-stirring concerts. In this way, he makes it possible for us to experience God and once again sense our own immortal aspects. Chamuel works together with the angels of music.

About This Theme

Many individuals feel at home in Chamuel's energy. It reminds them of their own angelic aspects, of the cheerfulness, playfulness, and easiness that many people remember from "another time before birth" and perhaps had still lived as children. Some people resign to the heaviness and toughness of the material world. Within themselves they have a deep knowledge that it is also possible to be easy and life to be cheerful. Yet, they experience the opposite time and again in reality: Nothing is created without effort and exertion, difficulties occur repeatedly, and states of pure joy and bliss do not last long. So they long for a place outside of this material world and want to return to the places of these memories.

However, this isn't the meaning of their life. People who have a strong sense of easiness within them and despair at the heaviness of the material world have often, as the theme of their lives, resolved to bring this easiness to earth. They want to discover how they can lead a pleasant, cheerful life and live harmoniously in joy with others. They want to create paradise on earth and share what they have learned with others. In order to do this, they must learn how to remain cheerful and calm, and still feel good, despite difficulties. They encounter the problems of life so that they learn how to easily resolve them.

Yet, the oppressive, constricting beliefs are often very strong. The troubles that arise time and again are no longer seen as learning steps and challenges, but as evidence that life is and remains difficult. People give up. However, if they do find the way, they will also become credible for others. Had these people received the easiness without ever having lived through strenuous situations and felt the despair and hopelessness themselves, they wouldn't be able to understand other people's problems. Their messages would be dismissed with the words: "That's easy for you to say, you've never been in such a situation." Only by experiencing this on their own and becoming successful in walking their own path they can show others the way.

When we have learned to create our earthly lives in a pleasant way, the longing for the otherworldly realms diminish. We recognize heaven on earth.

If we find our own convictions and patterns of belief that make our lives difficult, we have taken the biggest step. For example, the sentence "you can't trust other people" leads to tense and to be constantly on guard. Then it is difficult for us to hand over tasks to others. Consequently, we overburden ourselves with work and become stressed since we can't get everything done on our own. If we are forced to relinquish our work to others, we feel uneasy and other people often mess up the task that has been given them—because we expect this to happen and thereby create it.

There are thousands of examples like this. By looking inward time and again, by listening to the inner dialog, we can become aware of these limiting beliefs. If we remember our true being, our perfection and divinity, and once again connect with the love and abundance of existence—and use the power of the angels—these negative beliefs dissolve, along with the oppressive situations that evaporate like the fog when the sun shines.

Experiences

While working with the Chamuel energy, I recognized many of my limiting beliefs and attitudes about life. These patterns had made life difficult for me and attracted problems time and again. I frequently had "problem dreams" in which I completed tasks with great exertion. For example, I flew above a swamp area that turned out to be larger than I had expected. I could only reach the other shore with much effort and strain. I had not taken the easy path that led around the swamp.

At the same time, I experienced how easy it was to give up the limiting thoughts and feelings and quickly return to a stable, calm state despite sorrow, disappointment, and annoyance.

Many people have experienced the clarification of relationships within the family and with friends. One woman reported that she had reestablished harmony between quarreling members of her family while using the Chamuel Essence. They hadn't spoken with each other for years.

People often sense a loving and tender "warmheartedness," along with feelings of happiness, and contentment. They are calmer and more tolerant toward themselves and others. They are more spirited and have a positive attitude toward their lives.

Use in the Following Situations
- When the tasks or burdens of everyday life overwhelm you
- When there is no more room for joy, dance, and laughter in everyday life; for example, when you feel stressed by your children or overwhelmed by your work
- When you are constantly stuck in problems and feelings, or are joyless and depressive
- When you long for love and a sense of security
- When you feel unloved, deserted, or excluded
- When you no longer can laugh
- To clarify relationship problems
- When there are tensions in the family and partnership
- Also for love triangles—the angels do not judge, they use every situation to connect us with our own truth and consciousness and help us develop
- To prepare clarifying talks, even in business situations
- To resolve tensions with colleagues
- To form groups and to promote teamwork
- For creativity and inspiration
- To enjoy music

Works together with the energies of:
- the Ascended Masters Lady Nada, Kwan Yin, and Rowena
- the complementary Earthangel Air

Meditation

Perhaps you have at some time observed a hot-air balloon rising. Allow yourself to feel how such a hot-air balloon floats in the air. And while you experience the images and feelings, allow the energy of the Archangel Chamuel to envelop and fill you, just like the air fills the balloon.

The balloon is first attached to the ground and cannot rise until it has been filled with the hot, light air. The hot air that flows into the balloon makes it light, so light that it can fly and dance back and forth in the air. The balloon becomes larger and lighter through the air. Finally, the basket attached to the balloon begins to lift upward.

However, it cannot rise as long as the ropes hold it on the ground. It is still tightly moored, stuck on the ground, as if it were still heavy. Yet, when the ropes are untied, each of them loosen and let go. And the balloon with the basket begins to slowly lift into the air. It is carried and moved by the wind. And so your mood will also rise when you are filled with joy and love, when the energy of the Archangel Chamuel envelops you.

The balloon with its basket slowly glides higher until it has finally reached the point where it can go no higher. There is still ballast in the basket, and this ballast must first be thrown overboard before the easiness and the dance of the air can be experienced. Now allow yourself to throw your own ballast overboard. Recognize what has held you down in the heaviness of feelings and entanglements up to now and prevented you from dancing in cheerfulness and liveliness. Recognize why your mood, your inner feeling doesn't dance with life but feels weighed down or even crushed by the ballast.

And now throw everything overboard that you have already let go of, into the hands of the Archangel Chamuel so that the balloon—your mood, your sense of well-being—can continue to rise and let itself be carried by the easiness of the air and moved by the wind. In this way, the balloon will become free of ballast and its fetters. It simply rises up into the heights above the heaviness and the entanglements. And then it moves to the height that is exactly right for you in order to observe and enjoy life from a different perspective.

Gabriel

Beside Michael, the Archangel Gabriel is the best-known of the archangels. Not only he is mentioned in the Bible as a messenger—he proclaimed the birth of Jesus to Mary *(Luke 1.26-38)* and the birth of John (later called John the Baptist) to the aged Zacharias and his apparently infertile old wife Elizabeth—but also mentioned three times in the Koran[9]. Mohammed calls him the messenger of gods who dictated the Koran to him. Mohammed called him Gibril[14]. The Jews are also familiar with the angel Gabriel, considered one of the four Princes of Heaven[14].

Themes

Joy, happiness in life, hope, being reborn, resurrection, messages, expectations, wishes, desires, changes, freedom, "dying and becoming new."

Description of the Energy

The energy of the Archangel Gabriel is joyful, gives hope, feels like bubbly champagne, and is shiny and illuminating.

His name means: "God's strength," but is also translated as "God has shown himself"[14]. The main color associated with him is white.

General Tasks

Gabriel brings divine consciousness as joy, ecstasy, liveliness, and dance to earth. He also gives order to everything related to vibration, movement, and change: the vibrations of the atoms and the earth's vibrations and movements. *Schimmel*[9] writes "... and just like everything that has been created is involved in a continual dance, Gabriel also dances out of a love of beauty."

Gabriel serves renewal, resurrection, balance, and purity. He dissolves rigid structures. He accompanies every new beginning so that it is completed in harmony with the divine plan. The old form dies and changes into a new one.

Tasks for Human Beings

Archangel Gabriel is the angel of proclaiming resurrection. He brings the "joyful news," brings the Word of God to human beings and announces that something new and better will begin. He helps us recognize the next goal and our aim of life. His message sparks with joy because he is joy and reminds us that joy is an inherent, natural state.

People should happily orient themselves to what is new, even when this can suddenly change their entire life, as it did for Mary. He not only brings the message but also gives us the strength to accept and live the change and dissolve the rigid structures that prevent movement. In times of change, Gabriel stands at our side and gives us a perspective of the new.

The Archangel Gabriel not only proclaims messages but also helps us to understand visions and glimpses of the future. The future is often seen in symbols instead of concrete pictures. And the images of the unconscious mind are usually encoded and must be interpreted. Gabriel then stands at our side, just as he helped Daniel to understand his visions *(Daniel 8.16-27)*.

Gabriel brings joy into every situation, down into every cell of the body. As a result, the mood and level of vibration is elevated. He encourages us to dance with life and is especially effective in times of difficulty, depression, and hopelessness. Then he lets us again see the light-filled aspects of life so that we become optimistic and hopeful. When we dance with life, everything within us which is rigid and stuck becomes loosened. And we also become aware of the "hooks"—such as stress, annoyance, and fear—that pull us out of joy.

As the angel of proclamation, he also directs our eyes to our desires and frees us from constricting concepts, compulsions, and "not allowing ourselves, not being worthy." We learn to recognize which expectations and concealed longings block the way to a fulfilled life. While Haniel dissolves these limitations through clarity like a laser beam, Gabriel uses bubbly, warm spiritedness.

About This Theme

Wishes are the guides for the development of our being. *Kimberly Marooney* writes that "desire" actually means "de sire"—"coming from God." Wishes and desires show what is lacking for our fulfillment. They give us the strength to take the steps towards fulfillment and therefore helps us to develop ourselves. It is always helpful when we recognize and see what is behind our wishes—and not just on the spiritual path. The desire for a house of our own often has the wish for security behind it; the wish for a relationship is often the longing for love, completeness, and oneness. Some wishes that we expressed in the past are outdated. Yet, there are aspects within us that cling to them. As long as they slumber in the darkness of the unconscious mind, further steps will be blocked.

During the work with the essence of Gabriel, we received a large order. So Gerhard and I alternated worked at the labeling machine for two days: I worked until late at night and he began early in the morning. During this mindless work, I remembered that as a child I had wished for a job on the production line so that I wouldn't need to have any responsibility. Now I had the production-line work without any greater responsibility. I became aware that this wish to not bear any responsibility was still within me. The time to give it up had long passed.

Wishes can develop great power when we become aware of them and use them. The same applies to working with "I am" sentences and positive thinking. The "I am" sentences were created from a state of deficiency, from our own apparent imperfection, and we can replace them with the desired goal. "I don't have any money" becomes "I am wealthy." "I am in despair" becomes "I am hopeful." Longings, apparently the strongest form of wishes, are in reality blocks, especially when they are unconscious and we have suppressed them. While the wish is concrete and achievable, the longings are diffuse, elusive, and intangible. They are connected with the feeling that "this is so far away, so difficult, so rare that I will never receive it." As a result, they can hardly or never be realized and prevent us from living a perfectly fulfilled life.

When we take a closer look at our wishes and longings, they can be fulfilled and achieved. Or we may discover that they originated in an earlier time and have been outdated. Then it is easy to abandon them. Some wishes turn out to be illusions, expectations that are inappropriate. For example, there can be no fairy-tale prince or dream woman who can completely fulfill all of our needs. This wouldn't even be possible, if just for the reason that *our* needs are different and we change every day. The partner is a person with his or her own dynamic, which enriches the relationship. When we know exactly what we desire, the nebulous image of the fairy-tale prince or dream woman disappears and is replaced by something more concrete.

In situations of hopelessness, in which we can no longer see a solution, we often close the doors through which help and change could come. We feel like victims, helpless and abandoned, and nothing makes sense anymore. The resignation can be so deep that help may even be rejected or avoided. In such situations, if we succeed in hoping, in asking for a miracle (something that the logical mind considers completely improbable in this situation), the door will open for help and change. Blocked and stuck feelings start flowing again.

Experiences

During the time with Gabriel, I became aware of old expectations and wishes. Situations occurred that made me conscious of these outdated desires. I was "forced" to take an exact look at my wishes, not leave them in the diffuse fog but put them into concrete terms. In this process, I became clear about what was lacking and able to decide whether I wanted to continue working on their fulfillment or wanted to drop them. I worked with the sentence "I ask that all unfulfilled wishes and longings become conscious, that outdated wishes of the past dissolve, and that what fulfills me will enter my life."

Other people also reported that they precisely observed their situations and relationships. They asked themselves "what do I want, what do I get in this situation, and am I willing to pay the price of change?" Some felt sad or directionless. Others were tired and needed a great deal of sleep (processing in dreams). Many people felt joyful and light, capable of showing their feelings and letting them flow.

Use in the Following Situations
- To recognize and determine your goals in life and goals in general
- To formulate your wishes precisely
- In decision-making situations or if you are unfulfilled
- When there are changes
- Against hopelessness, depression, affliction, negative thoughts
- When you are stuck in destructive energies, even toward yourself
- If you feel locked in and rigid, against stagnation
- Gives consolation and new prospects in situations of change
- For healing the inner child
- For joy and dancing
- For clear and easy to understanding inner images, dreams, and visions

Works together with the energies of:
- the Ascended Master Pallas Athene
- the complementary Earthangel Sun

(Archangel Gabriel is traditionally associated with the element of water)

Meditation

The energy of the Archangel Gabriel is like the prickling of champagne, like the bubbling spring of joy that constantly overflows. Allow yourself to be filled with this bubbling joy and clarity. Imagine that your feet are standing in the bubbling spring of joy, which ceaselessly lets this power flow in colors or in a transparent form.

And like a flower, you can now absorb this joy, this bubbling power, and let it surge through your entire body. This source of energy flows through your legs into your pelvis, fills your abdomen, your chest area, and your arms up to your fingertips. It fills your back and bubbles along the spinal column up into your head so that it is also filled with the bubbling clarity.

Now allow this power to also flow through your aura and animate it with the feeling of prickling champagne. Observe the effect of the bubbling, cleansing energy and recognize where in your body and aura the bubbling joy can flow easily and where the power remains for a while in order to free the area of heaviness and disorders. At the conclusion, observe what it means for you to be completely filled with this divine joy. Ask this power to always appear when you need it.

Raphael

Themes

Healing, becoming complete, strengthening, renewal, transformation of the past, understanding the connection between illness—consciousness—soul, recognizing what we need to become healed.

Description of the Energy

The energy of the Archangel Raphael is soft, enveloping, healing, nurturing, clarifying, cleansing, constructive, renewing—like balm. It is both gentle and powerful. In the symbolic portrayals, Raphael also carries a vial with balm—because his energy is like balm for body, mind, and soul.

He is associated with the main color green. His name means: "God heals," "divine healer," or "God's medicine."

General Tasks

Raphael heals by restoring the divine order through the power of love, by connecting us once again with divine love. He nourishes and strengthens, which makes him responsible for every kind of healing, regeneration, rejuvenation, and renewal on earth and in the entire cosmos. He works together with the many angels of healing.

Raphael is also responsible for "healing between nations." He intervenes when the lives of people are injured by disorder, chaos, and war.

Tasks for Human Beings

Healing is also the Archangel Raphael's main task for human beings. He heals all areas of our being, not just the body but also the feelings, thoughts, situations, and our connection to God, to light, to oneness. When we have turned away from love or feel separated, his power makes it clear that love always surrounds and supports us, even if we do not notice it. All-encompassing love is like the sun that always shines, even when it is on the other side of the earth at night or hidden behind clouds and we cannot see it.

Raphael makes it clear to us why we believe we are separated from unity. He shows us the thoughts of separation behind emotional pain, burdening situations, or illness. Raphael's power connects with the power of love and restores order. As a result, the disorder, the malfunctioning of the body is regulated once again. His energy reaches down into the cells and the cell consciousness.

With his nourishing, loving, and gentle energy he also envelops people's feelings, as well as healing fear, mistrust, and "broken hearts." Since his focus as an archangel is the spiritual development, the connection to the divine, he makes us aware of spiritual learning steps behind illness and what we must do before we can become healed and whole.

In states of emotional shock, the energy of Raphael is like "balm for the soul."

"Every illness can be healed, but not every sick person." Sometimes the ailing are not willing to become healthy, even when they go to doctors and helpers. The illness brings them attention and care, or they use it to compensate guilt feelings. The power of Raphael helps in perceiving, in opening the doors for healing and then finding the right healer. However, he not only supports us in our healing but also in remaining healthy. We recognize the needs of our body, make sure we have the proper nutrition, clothing, protection, and stabilize our emotions. The power of Raphael frees us from obstructive thought patterns and attitudes.

Doctors and healers are often supported and guided by Raphael's power. Even if therapists do not notice it, his healing power also flows through them or guides their hands and thoughts. The same applies to the entire medical field—to orderlies, nurses, and the scientists who study diseases and search for new therapies.

Raphael shows us the path back to unity, to the origin from which we come. This is why he is sometimes called the "angel of the lost son." The doors of "the father" were never closed, and we were the ones who "went out" to the path. We only have to make the decision, then we will be reconnected with the power of the divine.

About This Theme

Whole and holy describe the same state, a condition that some human beings strive for: to be reconnected with the divine, with the unity, to be complete once again, to be whole. The saints are closer to this state than other people.

Behind every illness is a learning step. Many people are already aware of this and numerous books can help us in recognizing this fact. Yet, health disorders can also be healed even without the person learning the related step. I realized this at a seminar held by a Filipino healer. He worked with angels and cosmic doctors. He believed that the illness came from the Devil and God doesn't want us to be ill. Consequently, God was within the duality for him.

At first, I was astonished by this approach. However, I then recognized that even when the illness has been healed, the spiritual learning step still must be taken. If this doesn't occur at the same time as the physical healing and the person fails to find the necessary clue through "the miracle of healing," the theme will appear in another area of life, such as the person's relationship. Or the individual becomes ill again after some time has passed.

When I began to use these techniques myself, very little happened on the physical level. But things began "to seethe" and become conscious within the clients. I realized that the healer's orientation is reflected in his or her work. Physical healers have a great power in the healing of illnesses and can bring about "miracle healing." They are like car mechanics who don't care why the damage occurred; for example, whether the driver didn't pay attention to the oil level even though the warning light lit up. They repair the problem. Emotional healers have the gift of clarifying feelings. For spiritual healers, every healing—no matter whether it is physical or emotional—is related to a spiritual learning step. As long as the learning step is not completed or the client doesn't want to understand the root-problem, the illness usually remains.

In earlier times, spiritual healers were also called "healer priests." Spiritual healers work with the powers of the higher spiritual beings. Their goal is to bring human beings back into harmony with their soul's plan, with the cosmic order. This creates the preconditions for physical healing, and the symptoms of the illness usually also disappear after a period of time— unless these symptoms serve further understanding and learning steps. Some symptoms reveal a true treasure-trove of "aha" experiences.

Experiences

During the first days with the Raphael energy, memories from my past that hadn't been completely healed resurfaced. I remembered many situations from my childhood and had unpleasant dreams. Yet, the "charge" was resolved through this remembering. After a short time, I felt quite well.

The Raphael energy has been described by others as pleasant and calming, like the deep tones in music. They felt connected, accepted, and loved. They had a feeling of expansiveness, as if blocks melted away.

People reported that wounds in the relationships to their parents and partners also healed. They began to recognize and fulfill their own needs.

Use in the Following Situations
• When you feel separated from love, from God, from the origin
• When you feel lost, abandoned by God and the world
• When you are dissatisfied with yourself, with life and God

- When you are embittered and resigned
- For spiritual healing, to become one with yourself again
- For hurt feelings, love's pangs, and "a broken heart"
- For healing health disorders
- For supporting the willingness to heal
- To free yourself from limiting attitudes and thought patterns
- For regeneration and rejuvenation
- During menopause
- For helping those who heal, for doctors, healers, advisers, and researchers
- When you feel weak and exhausted
- To accompany the dying

Works together with the energies of:
- the Ascended Masters Mary, El Morya, and Lady Portia
- the complementary Earthangel Water

(In traditional literature, Raphael is associated with the element of air)

Meditation

Allow the energy of Raphael to embrace you, to flow through your aura and your chakras. This energy is like a balm that pleasantly touches and heals the painful areas. It gently hugs you, and your sore areas soak it up like a thirsty leaf absorbs the morning dew. Allow the balm to fill all of your aura and your entire energy system: not just the places that are sick, that are not in their natural order.

The balm has an agreeable effect on the entire system. The balm energy of the Archangel Raphael has the same pleasant effect as a massage with a nice fragrance oil.

And then allow this balm to also be soaked up by your skin, into the muscles and bones, into every organ, and into every cell. Everything that is sick in your body and has fallen out of the natural order is touched by this healing, regenerating energy. And all the other places are also nourished so that the natural, healthy order can once again spread throughout your entire body, connected with a feeling of well-being and relaxation.

Michael

Archangel Michael is one of the best-known and most frequently perceived archangels. He is mentioned in all three monotheistic religions: Christianity, Judaism, and Islam. His name also appears in ancient Egyptian mythology[14]. In the Koran *(Sura 2/ 92)*, he is called the representative of the divine will and distributor of food and mental abilities. He is described as a warrior, a fighter against the dark powers, as protection, and is often depicted with the blue flame sword. In the Bible, it says that many angels fight at his side *(Revelations 12.7)*. The 1st Hennoch book relates that he knows the secret oath through which the world was created and order established[14].

Themes
Clarity, purity, clarification, cleansing, protection, power, structure, willpower, taking action, courage, truth.

Description of the Energy
The energy of the Archangel Michael is clear, powerful, clarifying, and to the point, as well as protective, enveloping, and strengthening. His name means: "Who is like God?" He mainly is associated with the color of blue. I found him classified with the preparation "Phosphorus" in a homeopathy book.

General Tasks
As far as I know, Michael is the only angel whose name's meaning is a question. As an answer, he shows the path of every created thing: the path back to God. He accompanies us on this path. When beings face the question "Who is like God?," they once again orient themselves towards the divine.

Michael is the guardian of divine order. If, as mentioned above, he knows the formula through which the world, the duality, was created, then it is easy for him to maintain this order. Michael maintains the balance between the poles and intervenes in a regulatory manner when the play of the forces deviates from the divine plan. He uses his sword, which is symbolic of the clear power of love, to do this. His energy is not anger or battle in the human sense but clearly based in love. He is also called "God's executor."

Tasks for Human Beings

Michael accompanies human beings on their path between the poles of duality. He is effective when we become more and more lost in the darkness, in the forgetting, when we lose sight of "heaven."

Through his rousing question, *"Who is like God?"* he brings us back to the path of light, to the path of becoming conscious. Michael accompanies the souls of individuals into the forgetting and back out again.

Michael watches over our learning steps and whether we have enough strength to take our path. He is at our side in times of difficulties, when we have become entangled, or when we confront the dark pole. Then he protects us, strengthens our aura, and makes sure that the power of the dark pole does not exceed our own strength. He accompanies us on the entire path, even when we dare to go deep into the darkness or "evil" in order to have experiences. He keeps the path of return open for the soul. No matter how far someone has become distanced from God, the path back is never cut off since the divine force is ultimately at the core of our being. Without this divine spark, we could not live.

When a person is becoming conscious and is willing to learn and perceive, Michael uses his sword of love. This sword separates in order to create unity, it transforms the shadow and frees us from karmic entanglements.

In situations where we confront darkness or come into contact with it, he strengthens us and shows us the way. He can surround us like a protective mantle and strengthens aura and will, so that even oppressive outside energies (possession, elementals) must give way. He is always at our side. However, if we do not really accept his help, if we need to have certain experiences, or if we have not yet fulfilled our portion of the task, it is possible that we will undergo something unpleasant. Although this will not be harmful, it can strain us. People then draw the false conclusion that Michael's power isn't strong enough or that it is ineffective.

At a party, I once experienced how a handicapped man drained off my energy. He stood behind me and I felt dizzy and weak. Even though I moved to a different spot twice, this man followed me. I called on Michael for help and asked him to protect me. Although I immediately felt better, the protection was not as complete as I had otherwise experienced. I still kept losing energy. When I asked why I wasn't completely protected, he answered: "It is not a matter of protection this time but that you learn to stay in your heart and allow this man to receive the love that he needs through you."

This was difficult for me since I found him to be very unpleasant (which was naturally the best way to practice). Furthermore, I didn't feel like practicing that evening. I asked Michael to postpone the task and protect me. I immediately had my strength back and the man withdrew to the other end of the room.

Yet, the task was only postponed. The very next day, this man headed straight for me at our fair booth and stood next to me to ask about the essences and our work. My strength collapsed at first, but then I remembered the task. I opened my heart, allowed the love to flow, and accepted the man just as he was, with his unpleasant aura, with his way of drawing me close, demanding and wanting attention.

And then I recognized that his image of "I am a victim, you must help me" was so much focussed upon other people's energy that he could hardly absorb any of the cosmic power and love. He had become dependent upon other people's energy. At the same time, I also learned to draw the line and just give as much of the essences as felt right to me. I didn't follow my old pattern of being incapable of saying "no." This time, I was able to say "no" in a loving way to his demands while respecting and recognizing his path.

Had the protection provided by Michael the evening before been adequate, I would not have developed this ability. Now I can more easily deal with such situations.

As the teacher between light and shadow, Michael helps us to recognize and accept our own shadow aspects. Only then they can turn into light. He ultimately wants to accompany us in developing our own strength and will, the "Michael aspect" within us.

Michael is also called the guardian of karma. It is possible for him to clear karma and undo the karmic entanglements that we have with other people. He helps us recognize how entangled we are with the material world, with other people, and with the duality. He makes us aware of what we should give up to return to the unity. He helps us to recognize our own truth and stand up for it. He illustrates the divine will so that our will and the divine will can become harmonious.

Michael also strengthens our power to be sincere, capable of living our own truth. He dissolves doubt and fear, strengthens clarity, assertiveness, will, belief, and self-assurance. Ultimately, he enables us to be gentle and loving because we are aware of our power. Then we no longer must fight but can act in a calm and self-evident manner. We walk our path in a way that is upright and true to ourselves. We make no compromises. We stand up for our needs, even when fear paralyzes us or the opposing forces seem overpowering. We once again feel ourselves, have clear self-perception, leave the victim role behind, and assume responsibility for our lives.

Michael is the teacher for all aspects of power. Since his strength creates order and clarity, he makes it possible for us to create harmony and put our lives back in order. He gives us the courage to face challenges, no matter how difficult we think they are.

About This Theme

The Archangel Michael is the teacher on the theme of duality—"good and evil"—the basic theme of the dual world. This theme runs through all the myths, religions, and philosophies. It cannot be resolved by means of simple perception. Instead, it is a constant confrontation, an increasingly clear understanding, and a struggling for knowledge. This probably is why there are so many interpretations of Lucifer's fall.

If we remain in judgment, in black-and-white thinking, the story sounds like this: Lucifer wants to have the power for himself, wants to be like God, and rebels against God. This is why he is cast away from God and banished to earth. From here, he attempts to win his battle using any means possible.

The other variation is this: God wants to create the earth, the world of polarity. However, to do this he also needs the darkness in addition to the pole of light. Since there is no duality without both poles, there is no free will. Lucifer, the "light-bearer," also described as the angel who God loves the most, takes on this (thankless) task since no once else wants it. With his angels, he forms the dark pole. Why? Not because of a hunger for power, but so that human beings can have experiences in the field between good and evil. Here we can turn away from God, decide against the good, experience what happens if we separate ourselves from God, and learn how we can take the path back again.

Perhaps this theme is also symbolized by the Bible story of the lost son. The son (representing humanity) must first separate from the father, must go out into the world and experience poverty, pain, suffering, and pride so that he understands what he had possessed. After he has left his father's house, he must experience the unpleasant aspects of the duality. So he is tempted by the dark side and falls deeper and deeper into suffering, moving increasingly further away from paradise, from the unity. This continues until he has been banished from the world of human beings and suffers from hunger as a swineherd. Only then he recognizes what he had given up. Only then does he become aware of the love he had possessed and how happy he had been.

And when he reflects on all of this and returns home, he is immediately taken in by his father. His father holds a feast for him since he knows that this son has now perceived and become conscious.

The son who has stayed at home symbolizes the archangels and the angels, the beings of the spiritual world who have never lived in duality. They have never personally experienced what it means to be separated. They have always lived in bliss.

Don't we find the same happening in human life? Whenever things are going well for us, we usually don't appreciate it. We only become reflective when we lack what we need. Most people do not voluntarily set out on the spiritual path. Through pain, suffering, and illness do we begin to seek the meaning of life and God—or however we want to call the light-filled pole. Some people then learn to pray.

The dark pole has its task: it creates suffering, war, pain, illness, injustice, poverty, envy, violence, and tempts people into the darkness so that they perceive and change their ways—so that they once again seek the forgotten light and love. When we distance ourselves from the pole of light, we increasingly forget our origin and our true being. We separate ourselves from love. *Diabolus* means separate, break, and divide. On the way back into the father's realm, into unity, we integrate the suppressed shadow aspects and once again become whole.

Redemption takes place when we leave the area between the poles, the realm of duality, and enter the higher level of unity, the non-polarity (as described on page 29). Consequently, it hardly makes sense to judge and fight the pole of darkness. If we want to become healed and whole, we must also integrate our shadow aspects—which are reflected in the outside world.

The dark powers, the non-physical beings with whom some people are confronted, also have the same effect. For example, the so-called possessions with outside energies show that a learning step is overdue. Experienced therapists report that possessions always occur with the—of course unconscious—consent of the possessed person. Even when the possession has been resolved, if the affected person has not yet learned his lesson, it won't be long until another dark energy is attracted to the person (also see chapter on Elohim).

Dark powers have an unpleasant aura—and this is how people can perceive them: we get goose bumps, feel a spine-chilling shudder, or become afraid. Fear makes our aura thin and full of holes. As a result, we give the dark powers points to attach themselves and gain power over us.

Through Michael's strength, the aura becomes stabilized, our own power strengthened, and the connection to divine love intensified. If I don't want some other beings to make themselves at home inside of me and my house, this will not occur. We could say that these forces train our willpower and strength, just like weights train our muscles. If we have to learn this lessen, it may be that the trainer gives us increasingly heavier weights.

Sometimes we may read that the shadow powers primarily attack when we start the path towards the light. Then they attempt to force us give up the good intentions. (Flower A. Newhouse and Stephen Isaac: *The Christward Minister,* Ensondido, CA, 1st edition.)

My perspective is that the shadow powers intensify our own shadow aspects. There are various powers and desires, suppressed aspects within us that want to become conscious and be transformed. These become particularly visible when we set out on the path to the light. Some people are also afraid of evil because they fear losing their soul.

Some books even write that the guardian angel leaves us when we turn toward evil or the souls are disintegrated when they do not repent. These experiences come from the helplessness of childhood, the images of past centuries that still hover in the collective consciousness, or from past lives. In the past, these have been used as threats to keep people away from evil. Yet, the love of God accompanies us on our path and the guardian angel always stands at our side.

We only "play this game" as long as we move within the duality. The moment we wake up from our illusion of being separate and once again remember our true being, the illusion will collapse. It is like when we are at the movies and completely caught up in an exciting film: We suffer along with the characters. At the latest when the curtain closes, we wake up and return to the "normal" reality.

Archangel Michael is also the teacher for the theme of "will." The saying "not my will but thy will be done" is often understood to mean that I must set aside my will because God's will is better and more correct. This is the attitude of the child who fears being punished by the parents when it rebels against their will. But someone who is without a will has no power.

We have certainly all experienced the strength of a person (even a child) with a strong will. He achieves what he wants to achieve because he knows precisely what he wants and has no doubts about it. So the will helps us in attaining our goals. When we give it up, we give up a power that strengthens and advances us in life. The goal is not to give up our own will but to bring it into harmony with the divine will, the cosmic plan. Then our will and God's will are identical and we can use the power of the will.

Experiences

When I worked with the Michael energy, I felt strong and clear, full of energy. I began to work more effectively, to structure my day, to immediately take care of the pending tasks without postponing them like before. Together with the request to work on this theme, I received the inspiration of "separating from whatever keeps me from unity." As a result, many themes came to mind that had separated me from a fulfilled life. In addition, I confronted the theme of guilt feelings. While meditating with the Michael energy, I quickly received clarity and many things were resolved.

Other people also reported that they separated from old things. Some used physical cleansing methods like fasting or intestinal cleansing. Others cleaned the house.

Some noticed more clarity in their thoughts and words: "What I say hits the point and has an effect, people listen to me and take my words seriously. I can achieve things that had previously appeared unattainable to me. But I also have to take action. Something is expected of me," is what one woman who used the essence wrote.

One woman got stuck in an aggressive group of soccer fans—and even though she is a very fearful person, she felt safe.

Use in the Following Situations
- For stabilizing your aura
- When you feel weak, helpless, or like a victim
- Against self-doubts and the feeling of being incapable
- When you have nightmares
- In all situations where you to feel protected
- When you are exhausted
- When you feel threatened
- To recognize your truth and have the courage to stand by it
- When you saddle yourself with too much, dissipate your energies, or cannot create order in your life
- For your own discipline, order, and recognizing and creating structures
- To support people in leadership positions
- To free yourself from karmic attachments, compulsions, and limitations
- To cleanse your aura
- To cleanse and clear rooms and keeping them pure (therapists in particular report how they could free their rooms of oppressive energies with the essence in the morning and evening)
- To free yourself from outside energies
- For transforming destructive, aggressive, or hate-filled energies

- To strengthen your powers of discernment, to recognize dark powers and learn to deal with them
- In therapeutic work, for recognizing and separating from what is old or has been taken over from other people
- For beginning something new and ending something old, for completing something.
- To free you from opinions about yourself, you have taken from others

Works together with the energies of:
- the Ascended Masters Saint Germain and Djwal Khul
- the complementary Earthangel Fire

Meditation

The meditation with the Archangel Michael stretches over a number of days. Start with the earth chakra (also called earth star), the chakra located about 20—30 cm (8—12 inches) beneath the soles of your feet within the earth. The next day, direct the power of Michael into your foot chakras. The following day, direct it into your knees, and finally into the first chakra at the pelvis. Meditate every day with one chakra until you finish with the 8th chakra, which is located about 20—30 cm (8—12 inches) above your head (the 8th chakra is also called soul star). The following day, do the meditation of clarity before you start again with the earth chakra. You can clear your chakras of old patterns and karmic entanglements with this meditation journey.

Allow the energy of the Archangel Michael to envelop you, fill your aura layers, and strengthen your aura. And then let this power flow into your chakra. How does your chakra looks like? size, color, how active it is, the connection with the other chakras and the aura bodies; how well it provides the entire energy system with its energy. And then envelop the chakra with the energy of the Archangel Michael so that it becomes cleared and cleansed, once again returns to its original power and beauty, fulfilling its tasks in an ideal manner.

Allow this power to separate everything from you that no longer serves you: all the karmic entanglements, old patterns and feelings, and all the outdated self-images that do not correspond with your true being. Allow the power of Michael to separate what divides you from your true being and from oneness.

Let this power work until it has cleared the chakra to a degree that is correct and possible at this time. And then allow that this chakra, which is now cleared and connected with its original power, to be harmonious integrated into your energy system. Perceive how this chakra looks now: its size, its color, how active it is, and the connection to the other chakras and the entire flow of energy. And perceive how this feels for you now, how you feel with this cleared chakra and what changes within you as a result.

Meditation for Clarity

After you have cleared all the chakras during the past few days, starting at the earth chakra and up to the 8th chakra, allow the power of the Archangel Michael to harmoniously flow into these chakras so that they can work together in an optimal way.

Immerse yourself in your flow of energy, which flows from the earth chakra to the 8th chakra, and perceive how your aura is strengthened and begins to shine more brightly. The aura and the energy channels of the body become cleared and are freed of karmic entanglements as well.

Allow the energy of Michael to separate you from whatever divides you from your true being and unity so that your energy system becomes a harmonious, unified field. Extend yourself into your luminous being.

Jophiel

Integration, access to the higher aspects of being and consciousness, clarity, increasing awareness, self-realization, trust
God, powers of discernment, wisdom, steadfastness, divine
love.

Description of the Energy
The energy of Jophiel is gentle, integrating, and connective. We
feel ourselves surrounded by motherly warmth. He brings relaxation to situations in which we feel "pulled apart."

His name means: "God's beauty" or "God is my truth." He
works together with the angels of wisdom and has the color gold
associated with him.

General Tasks
Just as the light of the sun falls upon the earth and is available to
everything, Jophiel brings the divine light to all existence. This
is why he is also called the "angel of illumination." Like a ladder,
he connects the highest and lowest being, all levels of consciousness, and the spiritual and material world.

Information, ideas, perceptions, knowledge, wisdom, and
intellect flow through him, both to the earth and humanity, as
well as in the other direction. He builds bridges between the
various levels and dimensions so that impulses can flow. Spiritual beings can also enter the various dimensions through these
bridges. Angels come to earth and to humanity through these
bridges.

Ultimately, Jophiel connects us with the divine omniscience,
with what has always been and what is, and with the universal
truth. He teaches the power of discernment and accompanies
evolution and progress. Evolution means being oriented toward the highest consciousness and moving toward the highest
perception.

Jophiel is also the link to highest consciousness for human beings. If Metatron is the bridgehead, then Jophiel could be called the bridge. However, this bridge more closely resembles a ladder. It not only connects the two shores but also allows the various sections to connect with each other. This not only facilitates access to other levels of consciousness but also makes it possible for us to connect with our own higher aspects of being and aspects of our souls that have been split off. As a result, our perception and knowledge is deepened, and we can understand the correlations between earthly life and cosmic order. Jophiel also brings us visions. He links the crown chakra and aura with higher chakras and vibrational levels.

By connecting his own aspects of consciousness in other levels and expanding human consciousness, he helps us become complete. He accompanies researchers who seek correlations and knowledge, no matter whether these perceptions are of a spiritual, scientific, social, or business nature. As a result, he is also the companion of pioneers, discoverers, and inventors.

At the same time, he also teaches us to apply knowledge in harmony with the divine plan. This is how he also supports governments and communities.

Jophiel brings light into the dark hours of self-doubt, in which the connection to our inner strength and certainty is broken. He comforts us when we feel alone and small, when we feel that we are not part of life and cosmos. Then he directs the divine love towards us, strengthens the connection to our hearts, and dissolves the blocks.

He is like the greeting of divine love, which is called *namaste* in Sanskrit. Jophiel comforts us through this integrating, loving power.

About This Theme

Our human existence includes not only the body and the aura—we are also connected with higher levels of consciousness. Perhaps you have also experienced this with your higher self. At the beginning of our development, we feel that the higher self is outside of us and difficult to contact. We usually only succeed in this through meditation or with the help of special techniques. When we continue to develop our consciousness, this connection becomes natural and normal. The higher self with its knowledge and wisdom becomes a part of our everyday consciousness, as if the aura had expanded and included this aspect of being.

Then we no longer must go into meditation or apply techniques in order to use its wisdom. When we have a question and orient ourselves toward the higher self, the answer is there—in the form of a thought, a feeling, knowledge, or some other way that varies from individual to individual.

Just as the higher self is an aspect of us, there are also portions of consciousness and the soul in other areas and dimensions. For example, these can be found in the level of the ascended masters, the angels, and the archangels. In the beginning, we feel these aspects to be separate from us. But the more intensively we are in contact with them, the more they become integrated. So we increasingly have the feeling that they belong to us, just like our hair or toes are part of us.

I have experienced phases in which such an expansion occurred. I had previously had the feeling of "being beside myself" for a longer period of time—sometimes days, sometimes several weeks. I wasn't fully present, not completely in my power. I had a dull, hazy, unclear feeling. And then this foggy condition abruptly changed and I was once again myself, but different than before. I reacted differently, was stronger, and my previous difficulties had disappeared. For example, my way of making decisions had become more clear and occurred more quickly, even though I had been indecisive a short time before and frequently rejected the decisions that I had made. Sometimes I seemed to be standing next to myself and was astonished about how I had changed.

I have experienced that we have many concealed abilities. These are like presents that we haven't yet unpacked. Jophiel helps us in unpacking them and putting them to use.

The same also applies to the so-called split-off portions of the soul. We have separated with shock, pain, sorrow, or terror from some of our abilities, feelings, and aspects because of unpleasant, sad experiences or dramatic situations. For example, as a child I separated myself from the ability of perception. I was locked in the cellar and felt how an unpleasant force, an earthbound soul, came closer to me. In extreme fear and despair, I decided: "I will not see this" and suppressed the ability to perceive subtle forces, as well as other people's feelings. Later, I had to dissolve this block and integrate the split-off aspect in order to have the power I need for my work.

During the course of our spiritual development, many "I will never again..." phrases come up in relation to abilities, perceptions, and connections with other levels of consciousness that have been split off. Then it is time to heal the wounds and injuries and reintegrate what has been split off. The help of a therapist may be necessary for doing this work.

Experiences

Through the energy of Metatron, with whom I had worked before making the Jophiel essence, I had felt "pulled apart" and extremely tense. With Jophiel, I was instantly relaxed and felt well. I could also more distinctly perceive which abilities and aspects had not yet been integrated. I received the inspiration of, before falling asleep, very consciously extending an invitation to the aspects of my own soul that were still split off. Afterward, I received two treatments on this theme.

Consequently, I had the feeling that the higher levels of consciousness were accessible to me at any time. I became clearer, more conscious, and powerful.

Other people who worked with the Jophiel essence immediately after Metatron reported that they once again had both feet on the ground. They no longer felt as "light" and floating. They also recognized their "inadequacies," their abilities that they had not yet developed.

Some began to take a precise look at which aspects they were not living and had excluded from their lives. A person who used the Jophiel essence wrote how she discovered on New Year's Eve that she didn't have any party clothes. It became clear to her that she hadn't made a celebration out of her life; instead, she had buried joy in a deep pit. A few days later, she ran into her therapist, made an appointment, and invited joy, movement, humor, and beauty back into her life. She fixed up her apartment and found contentment within herself.

Another person who used the essence reported that after being trained in a new technique, she was unusually quick in starting to use it. She stopped reading about additional theoretical knowledge and enjoyed doing the practical work.

Use in the Following Situations
- When you want to learn or have problems with learning
- For visions and inspirations
- To come into contact with inner wisdom
- To strengthen your contact with intuition, the inner voice, and the higher self
- When you have to take examinations
- For science, perception, understanding
- Against ignorance, lack of awareness, pride, and narrow-mindedness
- When you get lost in thoughts and fantasies, when you no longer can differentiate knowledge and wisdom from untruth and imagination
- When you feel unclear and confused
- When you feel torn by inner conflicts, to take the tension from the body
- To learn and integrate new abilities

- To solve problems
- For inner peace

Works together with the energies of:
- the Ascended Masters Hilarion, Orion, and Sanat Kamakura
- the complementary Earthangel Crystal

Meditation

Jophiel now invites you on a journey to other aspects of consciousness. First focus on your feet, your legs, and let your attention travel along your chakras to the 7th chakra, which is at the top of your head. Perceive how each chakra is different and vibrates in a different way. Then let yourself be carried by Jophiel's power into the 8th chakra, which is located about 20—30 cm (8—12 inches) above your head. And then go further up into other chakras and dimensions.

Allow the Archangel Jophiel to accompany you to exactly that portion of consciousness that wants to contact you and perhaps reconnect with your current consciousness. Make contact with this aspect or this chakra. What do you perceive? How does it feel? Which images, feelings, or information does this area contain? And then allow yourself to extend into this aspect of your being and merge with it.

Now you can integrate these aspects into your earthly consciousness, if you want to—either now or later, completely or just one portion of it. And then allow this aspect of your being to integrate itself as much as you want and as much as is right for you. Observe what happens and what changes. You are more than the body. You are more than the thoughts and feelings. Your perfect being is all-encompassing. Allow yourself, little by little, however it is right for you, to grow into this being. And allow the Archangel Jophiel to accompany you.

And then shift your attention back to the here and now, to your body and breathing, and move your hands and feet.

Zadkiel

Themes

Perfection, wisdom, knowledge, connecting with the energy of the divine force, redemption, freedom, complete cleansing and development, leaps in consciousness, bliss, stillness.

Description of the Energy

The energy of Zadkiel is integrating, harmonizing, and balancing. It connects "Heaven and Earth," and expands at the same time. Just like plants grow, we extend ourselves "upward," in breadth and in depth. The energy of Zadkiel has a relaxing effect and frees us from limitations, imperfections, and feelings of being tied down.

Violet is the main color with which the Zadkiel energy is associated. His name means "God's goodwill."

General Tasks

The task of the Archangel Zadkiel is to extend the divine structure into the earthly realm, the duality. He develops the highest potential of every being, the perfect form, the perfect nature, and the perfect structure. As a result, he also contains the possibility of extending beyond the momentary structure into the next level, in the next dimension. Just like a citrine develops from an amethyst, just like coal can turn into diamonds under the right conditions, he also brings every being to the perfection of form and opens the possibility of transformation into other forms.

Zadkiel is the angel of growth, of development, of completion. Everything that has been created bears the ideal form within itself. It follows a divine plan and attempts to develop itself into its perfectly completed form here on the earth. This applies to crystals and diamonds, as well as animals and human beings—it applies to every form of existence. Zadkiel also supports the fairy kingdom and the realm of the devas and nature spirits so that the plants, animals, and the "stone world" can develop into their perfect form.

Zadkiel is also the "guardian of the cosmic laws," the laws of what always has been, is, and always will be. He creates the harmony of all being with the cosmic principles, ultimately with the principle of love. Like a strict teacher, he watches to make sure that these principles are learned and adhered to.

Tasks for Human Beings

Zadkiel connects people with their potential, with their divine aspect and perfect being. He not only allows us to become conscious, but also shows the paths of how to live this awareness and extend it into everyday life. We connect with our power and the higher knowledge. All aspects are brought together. Whatever had previously prevented us from integrating these aspects is resolved.

The term "purification" aptly describes his work: We develop our pure being, live without the veil of forgetting, without fears or old limitations. At this point, new dimensions of being, of life, open up.

Zadkiel's power has the effect of fine-tuning to the divine, the perfect. When other themes have been resolved and the other angels have done their work, Zadkiel harmonizes the last imbalances and prepares the transition to the next learning step, the next level, or the next plane. This ultimately leads to us experiencing ourselves and living in every situation.

Zadkiel is also called the angel of invocation, of prayer. In prayer, we ask for divine strength and attune ourselves with the frequency of the divine. And, as in meditation, in prayer we also bring our divine, light-filled aspects back into harmony with human existence. Then we have more strength to carry this with us into everyday life.

Zadkiel inspires the people who create or want to compre-hend the rules, laws, structures, and principles. As a result, his power can support politicians, judges, engineers, scientists, and architects.

About This Theme

Perfection is not perfectionism. We often have exact ideas about how something should be and when it would be perfect. And this is how we trip ourselves up or waste our energy. We do not recognize that something is already perfect because we are still waiting for it to become how we imagine it should be. We plant a seedling and expect a lilac to blossom. Instead, a rose grows and we wait for it to finally turn into a lilac.

Perfection is a state within the cosmic framework. Even if we believe that something is not perfect, it still may be perfect. We are not perfect either. We still have many rough edges and patterns that conceal our true being—and yet our being is complete.

The key to understanding is love. No matter whether we are dealing with other people, the laws of nature, plants, animals, crystals, scientific principles, or the cosmic order—through love we put ourselves into a state of harmony. Love listens and perceives with the heart.

This way of understanding opens other perceptions and correlations than when we only want to understand with the rational mind and logic. With the key of love and "coming-into-harmony," we have access to all knowledge, no matter whether it is related to the healing power of plants or the knowledge beyond time and space.

Experiences

When I worked with the Zadkiel Essence, it became easier for me to turn what I had perceived into concrete reality. I was disciplined and didn't let myself become discouraged as quickly.

People who worked with the power of Zadkiel felt more balanced and calm. At the same time, they also felt clear, strong, and guided.

Use in the Following Situations
• For self-assurance and clarity
• In all growth steps and challenges

- In order to integrate *and* live all split-off portions of the soul, portions of consciousness, and shadow aspects
- Against the fear of recognizing your abilities and putting them to practical use
- To transform negative states and limitations
- When you can't let go and cling to annoyance, limitation, a small self-image, and feelings of unworthiness; when you don't want to see or ignore experiences that block or even inspire you
- To create supportive structures and rules
- To recognize principles
- To reconcile your life with your life plan
- For meditation, stillness, calm thoughts

Works together with the energies of:
- the Ascended Masters Victory, Lao Tse, and Helion

Meditation

Let yourself be enveloped by the power and energy of the Archangel Zadkiel. Allow this energy to flow through your entire body and nourish you. And then allow the Archangel Zadkiel to carry you into the light of perfection. Safe in his unfailing arms, you immerse yourself in this light. It envelops you, fills your aura, your entire body.

It dissolves the resistance you have to yourself and dissolves the dissatisfaction with your situation. It touches the divine spark within you. The light of perfection strengthens and fortifies your divine spark, and gives it the power to extend, to take up more space, to become as large as is right for you. Now it's possible to perceive, feel, comprehend, and live your perfection. The light of perfection stabilizes the divine spark within you so that it even remains alive in the storms of everyday life and continues to grow.

And now let yourself be carried into the here and now on Zadkiel's arms. Feel your body, your perfection, and the divine spark within you.

Metatron

As the name already implies, Metatron is a special archangel. His name doesn't end in *el* like the others do. This is why he is not included with the archangels in other systems. He is often called the Prince of the Angels or the King of Angels. He has the highest vibration of the archangels and is closest to the origin within the hierarchy of the archangels. He is the guardian of the threshold between form and non-form. While Uriel stands on the side of the material world on the bridge between the divine and the earthly, Metatron forms the opposite bridgehead. Like Melchizedek, Metatron is said to have been a human being at one time.

Themes

All-encompassing love, perfection consciousness, opening the gates of consciousness, stillness, "everything is," connection to our own divinity.

Description of the Energy

His energy is fine, gentle, and clarifying. It is pure, all-encompassing love. The colors white, mother-of-pearl, and gold are associated with him.

General Tasks

Metatron is the beginning and the end, Alpha and Omega, the birth of the light from the divine void, from the unity. As the guardian of the threshold, Metatron gives form to the ideas of possibilities. Behind him is the space of the void, the space in which all possibilities are contained. Within this space, the visible light also disappears since there is nothing there that could reflect the light. This is why velvety darkness sometimes appears when we immerse ourselves in the Metatron power. Or sometimes a radiant white light appears, the light that is still unified. Just like a prism, Metatron divides the white light into different colors and dissolves the energy of unity into separate parts.

His power is the power of love, the love that creates everything and is active within everything, the power of God. Through this love, the possibilities are given form. However, matter is not yet created. On this level the vibration is not yet so condensed that matter could arise.

The effect of Metatron can be compared to the work of the mind: thoughts, images, visions, and ideas suddenly arise out of "nothing." These ideas are then thought out shaped (the archangels and angels do their work here) and then manifested in more solid forms. Then they are turned into matter (which is the task of the numerous angels of manifestation, the nature angels, and human beings).

Metatron participates in the creation of all things. He accompanies the creation of the universe, of planetary systems, forms of development, social structures, and progress. The same also applies to the creation of the spiritual world, the archangels, angels, and other spiritual beings. He also helps in the "birth" of souls and group souls, which is when the souls become individuals, when they leave the unity—when the drop in the ocean becomes a drop on its own.

Together with Melchizedek, he translates the impulses of the divine force into solid terms. He is in charge of the more intellectual, spiritual aspects while Melchizedek is at the top of the materialization ray (see illustration "The spiritual Hierarchy", page 28). At the same time, he makes it possible to return into the unity, into nothing. He dissolves the forms when it is time to do so and brings them back into the void. The drop becomes one with the ocean again.

Metatron is also the angel of transition. He helps in every transition, in every change of vibration, and—in our current age—especially in the intensification of vibrations.

Tasks for Human Beings

Metatron also opens the doors of human consciousness and human dimensions. He enables us to experience perception, clarity, and insights. He opens our eyes for what is essential. Through his energy, we once again touch the unity. He shows us that human beings, even if they are still in the body, can merge with God or the divine force. So Metatron is also one of the most important companions on the path of initiation. Through his energy, we recognize what could be and what is an obstacle on our path. We perceive who we are, how we could live, and resolve hindering blocks.

Metatron lets us recognize the various paths and possibilities, as well as the consequences that result. And so we can comprehend that each day, life itself offers a path of initiation when we understand how and make use of it.

Metatron connects us with the power of love and opens the human heart. His power usually brings stillness, contentment, bliss, unity, and all-encompassing, non-emotional being. His power increases consciousness and vibrations. It meets human beings where they are and brings them into the higher realms.

When we work with his energy, we should be well grounded because we may otherwise lose the contact to the ground and the body.

About This Theme

The space of the void, the possibilities, is the realm in which everything exists but has not yet been brought into form. It is not yet separate and not yet differentiated. We can compare it to an empty piece of paper upon which everything can be written or drawn. This piece of paper bears all possibilities within itself. Yet, the lines must still be drawn to make them visible. This example also makes it clear that the space of possibilities does not contain invisible forms and ideas. The house that I want to build does not already exist there as an invisible form. The letter that I want to write also does not exist on the paper and does not just need to be traced. Within the space of possibilities, there are no seeds that only have to become visible and grow. This would all be form that is just invisible.

Within the space of possibilities, everything is contained, everything is possible, and only an impulse is required to assume form. We can compare this to an empty piece of paper: It gives us the opportunity of writing a letter, but the impulses and the words come from the writer. However, the letter would not be possible without the paper.

Metatron is not the writer—the writer is God, the divine force. But we can also be the writer when we create things with our thoughts and impulses and give form to our visions. Metatron is the midwife at the birth.

Just as everything has separated from the space of possibilities, from the unity, in order to come into existence, the human soul also separates itself like a drop from the ocean. During meditation or regressions, when I immerse myself in the birth process of the soul, I experience each time that this birth was extremely painful for me. It was the pain of separation, of being split off from the unity, of being thrown out of paradise so that perception—the knowledge that we gain through the tension of the two poles—becomes possible.

I feel this pain of separation each time when there are separations in my life, no matter whether this is a separation from a partner, from someone who has died, or from material things that I have grown to love. Ultimately, the pain of separation from the unity is always the basis of this pain. The more I can resolve this pain, the more I recognize that I am no longer separate but still a drop in this ocean, the more this pain of separation also heals. And I love this earthly life more and more. Metatron has helped me in attaining this goal.

There is a very special protection in Metatron's energy. Other than the protection through white light, through a mantle of light, or through strengthening the aura (by Archangel Michael, for example), Metatron lays a mantle of love around us. This mantle does not keep away "evil" but its love transforms things. Love is the power that lets non-form become form and vice versa.

This mantle of love neutralizes the duality: Good and evil are no longer in effect. He lets us recognize that good and evil are only two aspects of one energy and that both have the same goal: both lead us back to the origin. When we are in the love, we can accept the evil in love and it dissolves as a result. Love also dissolves the fear that makes holes in the aura and cuts us off from the light of the origin. In this mantle of love, there is no longer good and evil. Everything that immerses in it becomes love.

However, this protection can only be used by people who have internalized that good and evil are the poles of the duality and that this division does not exist outside of duality. It is protection for people who can accept the evil in themselves and in the outside world. It is for people who no longer must protect themselves against evil because they have recognized that the dark side is also within themselves and wants to be accepted and loved. Only then our vibration is high enough to connect with the power of Metatron as protection.

The power of Michael is better suited for people who want to protect themselves against the evil or in situations when we need a protective mantle. Michael stabilizes the aura and forms protection like a safeguarding shield. However, Metatron's power can be used to understand duality and unity, good and evil, and everything beyond, and achieve the state of love.

Experiences

Many people report that they were "pulled out of the body" during the connection with the Metatron energy. Consequently, it is good to ground ourselves when we work with this energy or simultaneously connect with the energies/essences of Tree or Sanat Kumara. The essence of Metatron should be used in moments of stillness and meditation, but not while driving a car or during activities that require presence of mind.

Some people feel the Metatron energy to be oppressive: They become nervous because the vibrational level is too high for their momentary condition.

Through the energy of Metatron, people enter a state of stillness, peace and quiet, and a space beyond everyday life. I also experienced this. At the same time, a feeling of love without intention flooded my being. I felt myself filled with the warmth of the heart and experienced life as light. I could have embraced the whole world at that moment.

The physical feeling I got after working "too long" with the Metatron essence was just like a rubber band that is stretched and stretched until it threatens to break. It became physically unpleasant for me.

Many blocks were dissolved at a speed that I had never before experienced, even if the old patterns weighed on me once again at the start. Feelings of "I don't want to do this anymore, everything is so difficult" oppressed me again.

Yet, at the same time, I received clear messages in my dreams and experiences. For example, I dreamed that I was invited to a meal. A group of people stood around the cook and watched him make the last motions in the preparation. All that was missing was a dash of cream. A delicious fragrance already filled the room. But, just before the meal was ready to be served, the cook said: "I'm not in the mood anymore" and threw everything in the trash can.

This dream showed me that I already had achieved a great deal in my life. But still I had the tendency to throw everything away because I believed it would never be "ready."

During this time, I once again had worked too much and overexerted myself. My most ardent wish was "to not do anything anymore."

One day, I had a little time before a seminar. In a cafe, I observed an old woman who no longer had anything to do. I felt how, when she got up in the morning, she wished that the day would already be over. She had no purpose in her life. This made me realize that I had too much desire for action within me to "no longer do anything." What I really wanted was a break and recuperation. And I realized that I ultimately want to take action without having the feeling of doing something that exhausts me.

"Simply being" does not mean laying in bed and no longer moving but taking action without intention and being in harmony with existence. The feeling of "I want" dissolves and I do what needs to be done. I began to allow myself things that were good for me: massages, baths, and time in the sun.

Use in the Following Situations
- When you feel separated from God, from the unity
- For meditation
- To connect with all of existence and with the core of your being
- To connect with the love of the heart and all-encompassing love
- To recognize the possibilities and the path
- When you need clarity
- For people who live in a world view that is too narrow, who cannot see the possibilities and miracles of life, who are materialistic, who are cut off from others and from existence
- Against depression
- To support those who are dying

It should *not* be used when you must be active or speak since the energy of Metatron lifts people out of everyday life.

Metatron doesn't directly work together with an ascended master.

Works together with:
- the complementary Earthangel Melchizedek

Meditation

Let yourself be carried by a spiral of light. Slowly and lovingly, the white or colored light carries you higher and higher into silence, into the space of the void, into the space of possibilities. On Metatron's arms, you are transported up into this space of unity. And on his arms, you are safe and secure as you immerse yourself in the origin of all being, in velvety blackness that contains everything and is also your origin.

Allow yourself to expand within this space, as far as is right for you at the moment and merge with this space of possibilities.

Then, after a while, pull yourself back into your present form and let Metatron's arms carry you back, down the spiral to your body, into the here and now. Move and feel yourself in your body.

The Earthangels

Melchizedek is not one of the earthangels. Yet, he is described here because his position is at the top of the materialization ray. He sends the divine impulses on to the earthangels. The Earthangels Crystal, Tree, and Sun form the higher order, while the earthangels of the four elements resonate at a lower frequency than the first three.

The earthangels of the four elements are not the elements themselves but the angels in charge of them. They lead the impulses to the respective nature spirits and into the elements. These angels are not the forces, so that human beings have worked with in shamanism or during past centuries. They are the balancing creative aspects of these qualities, which bring us into harmony with these forces. The earthangels teach us how to use them in order to develop and perfect ourselves. They teach us the joy of life through the forces of the elements.

Melchizedek (also Melchisedech)

Melchizedek is quite unknown in our current age. When we first came into contact with his energy, we were surprised at the power and strength that he radiated. We recognized him as the force that directs the materialization ray (see page 26).

Melchizedek was already mentioned in the Bible, both in the Old and New Testament. He was the priest and king of Salem, the present-day Jerusalem, during the time when the city served the Ammonite deity. He was called the priest of the "Most High God."

In the New Testament, Jesus is associated with the order of Melchizedek: "Jesus has gone as a forerunner on our behalf, having become a high priest for ever after the order of Melchizedek" *(Hebrews 6.20)*. In contrast to other high priests, Melchizedek was both a priest and a king. Consequently, he not only assumed spiritual tasks like many priests before and after him but also united the spiritual and material tasks. He was the priest of the Most High God and simultaneously the ruler of the material realm. That Jesus was also placed in his order (succession) shows that Jesus also assumes the task of bringing spirituality and everyday life into harmony.

Melchizedek is called the king of righteousness and peace in the New Testament *(Hebrews 7.2)*. The next verse says that "He is without father or mother or genealogy, and has neither beginning of days nor end of life, but resembling the Son of God he continues a priest for ever." There have been more priests in his tradition and a priest order of Melchizedek was created.

Description of the Energy

When we come into contact with Melchizedek, we encounter an infinite power and might. It appears to have no boundaries, everything is possible and everything can be created. While Metatron represents this energy in the spiritual realm, we can feel that this also applies to the material world for Melchizedek. Although his energy is very powerful, he is also full of love and peace.

General Tasks

Together with his helpers and the angels, Melchizedek translates the divine impulses into concrete reality. Just as Metatron is the highest archangel, Melchizedek is the highest being of the materialization ray (see illustration "The spiritual Hierarchy", page 28). He absorbs the divine impulses and leads them into the material form. This means that he has participated in the creation of the earth, human beings, the galaxies, and the entire universe, the entire Creation. He rules over all knowledge, all wisdom and perception.

Just like he participates in creation, he also watches over adherence to the divine order so that nothing deviates from the plan. In addition to the earthangels, healers and cosmic physicians also belong to his ray. Among other things, they work on the healing and preservation of the earth, intervene in natural catastrophes, and presumably also regulate some of the damage that occurs to the earth because of human carelessness.

Although Melchizedek and his "employees" maintain the equilibrium of the earth, we should not conclude that we are excused from our duties and responsibilities as a result. It's time for us human beings to learn to accept responsibility for our actions, to look ahead and see what consequences our actions will have, and to preserve the earth.

"Subdue the earth" is what is said in the Bible—and this means that we human beings have had the responsibility for the earth. As long as we did not have a clear view of the consequences of our actions, we received help. But do we know whether the catastrophes of recent years are an indication that we now must know more and do more? And who knows what the plans of God are? It is possible that this place could be destroyed if we human beings don't learn to take care of the planet earth. Even this would be an experience for our souls.

Tasks for Human Beings

Melchizedek and his angels support us to assume responsibility for the world and live in harmony with it. He is a teacher and mediator in this age. He brings spirituality and the material world, "divine service" and everyday duties into harmony. He can show us the way to live in harmony with the world. Therefore, he is called the king of peace.

Melchizedek is a priest-king. And so he teaches us to live our spirituality in everyday life. We are the co-creators and also possess power. Melchizedek can teach us to accept our power and to create and rule in harmony with the cosmic plan, as well as in love. He imparts knowledge and perception to us, shows us how to fulfill these tasks, and guides us. He helps us to develop our love for the earth and the material world, enjoying our tasks and learning steps. And, as previously mentioned, this does not just relate to the material world but also to spiritual development and the harmony between the body, soul, and mind.

Melchizedek not only teaches harmony with the earth, but also harmony with the body. His power strengthens the connection between body, mind, and soul. He shows us how to grow in harmony with the body and our own being. Together with the Archangel Raphael, he serves the healing of the body. He strengthens the will to live and the respiratory system.

Use in the Following Situations
- To bring spirituality and everyday life into harmony
- To develop your own power and strength in love
- To strengthen your creating power
- For spiritual teachers
- For leaders and leadership tasks
- For politicians and national leaders
- To accept and love your body
- To heal the body, particularly together with the Archangel Raphael
- For healing father issues

- When you are angry at existence, at God
- For healing the earth
- When you have resistance to the material world, to life on earth
- To understand material correlations, for science and research
- For developing new technologies that support the environment (and aren't just tolerated by it)

Works together with:
- the Christ power
- the complementary Archangel Metatron

We received the message that people in meditation and in the midst of everyday life should immerse themselves in the Melchizedek energy. This energy is not (yet) available as a LightBeings essence, which means, not bound to a material carrier substance.

Meditation

Relax in your favorite way. Or, for example, by observing the flow of your breath. Observe how you inhale and exhale and how your chest rises and falls as you do so.

And while your entire body relaxes more and more, the energy of Melchizedek surrounds you like a golden sphere of light. At first, it only touches the outer layers of your aura...and then it increasingly fills your aura bodies...until it finally touches your skin. Perceive what qualities this energy holds for you today—is it light or heavy, strong or gentle, how does it feel, does it perhaps have a fragrance?

And then this golden energy also touches your body, fills the skin...the muscles...all of the organs...the bones...down into every cell...until it finally meets the sphere of light within you, your center. Perceive how your own sphere of light feels, how it looks, what color it has, and what happens when it is touched by Melchizedek's energy. And then allow the Melchizedek energy to strengthen the sphere of light within you...

Then take a deep breath. Be present and strengthened in the here and now.

The Earthangel Crystal

Themes

Connecting higher consciousness and resonance with the body, clarifying the crystal structures in the body, stable structure, constancy.

Description of the Energy

The energy of the Earthangel Crystal is light, clear, balancing, calm, solid, and comparable with a diamond or a pure herkimer crystal. It integrates, clarifies, and creates a different understanding of time.

General Tasks

The Earthangel Crystal has the ability to connect high spiritual vibrations with matter, to bring divine spirit into the material world. And he is always involved when matter becomes endowed with a living soul. He connects crystals and gemstones with the spiritual beings who work through them. He connects the planets with their own spiritual nature. He connects trees with the nature of the trees. He supports to find the ultimate form, a stable structure that can be maintained with little energy. And the Earthangel Crystal clarifies structures.

Tasks for Human Beings

Just as the Earthangel Crystal connects gemstones with spiritual beings, he also helps the body adjust to higher vibrations and levels of consciousness. This occurs in particular when he cleanses the crystalline structures of the body from strains, painful experiences and memories that are stored in the bones, muscles, and cells. Consequently, his energy is also helpful in clearing and regulating bodywork like Rolfing, cranio-sacral therapy, and massage.

Crystal stabilizes the inner structures, brings them into a stable order, and makes them receptive to higher vibrations and energy as a result. In particular, the crystal energy effects the skeleton and crystalline structures of the cells. Then, the higher vibration becomes anchored and harmoniously integrated into the body, bringing the entire body to a higher, more stable energy level. This makes it possible for life energy, *prana*, and other supportive cosmic energies to more easily become absorbed. The cleansed crystalline structures resonate more easily with the higher vibrations. If the crystalline structures are not cleansed, a dissonance occurs during the adjustment to the higher vibrations.

This force supports that beauty and individuality of the soul, is also expressed through behavior, thoughts, and the physical body.

The energy of Crystal brings inner calm and serenity by creating a different sense of time. Just as a crystal forms a structure that grows slowly and lasts for a long time, we can also observe what happens around us with inner serenity and peace.

The crystal lattice is a stable, lasting order that needs no energy for its preservation. And so Crystal can teach us how we can create lasting order within our surrounding world and ourselves: For example, instead of throwing the piece of paper in a drawer, we file it and put the file in the appropriate place.

When we connect with crystals and look at their beauty, or when we explore crystal caves, we are close to this divine principle in the world of nature. By immersing ourselves in this structure, we experience and comprehend what this divine principle means.

About This Theme

Through practicing subtle techniques and during times of an energy change towards a higher vibrational level, the subtle body adapts more quickly to the higher energy level than the more condensed physical body. Because of the increased discrepancy in the energy of these two bodies, we experience various symptoms like tension, pain, illness, high sensitivity to light and noise. And the more disorders and deposits burden the physical body, the more severe these symptoms will become.

In addition to specific energy work or meditation, we also come in contact with higher vibrational energies in other ways. The energy level of the earth has been constantly increasing in recent years. This does not take place continuously, but on certain days. On these days, a conspicuously large amount of people suffer from the described symptoms without a visible cause. Sensitive people who perceive these changes feel when they are "in the air." On such days, the essence Crystal works like a balm.

According to Gabriel Cousens, the entire human body is an interdependence of oscillating solid and liquid crystals that form an extensive energy pattern for the whole body. The skeleton is like a massive crystal with the ability to transform vibrational energy such as sound and light into electromagnetic and electrical energy, which it even directs down to the level of the cells.

The cells also have crystalline qualities and are viewed as liquid crystals. Liquid crystals are structures that possess the qualities of a liquid, store information, and have a measurable electromagnetic field. They can behave like a liquid, yet still be like a crystal at the same time.

In a healthy body, the crystalline structures resonate harmoniously with each other. They mutually influence each other. If this synchronicity is lost and intensive disharmony occurs, the body becomes ill. If the crystalline system is brought back into balance, the disharmony heals.

Cousens writes that the crystalline bone structure is an antenna for all external and internal information and vibrational energy. It intensifies this information and sends it on to all of the cellular and sub-cellular systems. When there is an increase in the vibrational frequency as a result of energy work or through intensification in the earth's energy level, this change is absorbed through the crystalline bone structure and transmitted down to the level of the cells. If the bone structures are already dissonant because of something like spinal trauma, for example, this will be activated by the increase of vibrations. Old symptoms may occur again. A clarification of crystalline structures can have a harmonizing effect on the entire body system.

Experiences

People who worked with the energy of Earthangel Crystal seemed to be surrounded by a bright crystalline glowing and sparkling. Although a few individuals felt this to be "cold," others sensed it as delicate and soft. Many people had less hunger and ate less. I always use the Crystal Essence when I sense tension and conflict in my body. This is especially intense when the vibration increases. The Crystal energy then has a relaxing and clarifying effect.

One woman reported that she felt more balanced and calm, and no longer became so stressed, because of the Crystal energy. Now she used the LightBeings Crystal Essence before situations that were formerly stressful for her.

However, people who are poorly grounded had difficulty in keeping their feet on the ground. Consequently, it is good to be well-grounded when using this essence.

Use in the Following Situations
- To integrate a new, higher energy vibration in the body
- In times of external increase in vibrations
- To clarify old patterns and energy structures, even in the cell memory
- To cleanse and clarify the crystalline structure of the body
- After cleansing or cathartic techniques, to fill the freed area with clear light
- When you suffer from inner conflicts and feel tense
- To support the absorption of *prana*
- In stress situations

- When you follow the *Living on Light* approach (Jasmuheen) to nourishment
- To optimally support your posture
- To come into harmony with crystals and gemstones and understand their vibration, energy, and message
- To heal crystals and gemstones

Works together with:
- the complementary Archangel Jophiel

Meditation

In the way best suited for you, relax and invite the energy of the Earthangel Crystal to envelop you. Perceive this energy, feel how you sense this energy, and see what color and what qualities it has...

And while the Crystal energy increases, allow that it slowly and gently flows through your crown chakra, which is located in the middle of your head, into your body.

Perceive how the Crystal energy lovingly flows into your bones. It first streams through your cranial bone, jaw bones, as well as your teeth. As it does this, it cleanses and clears your bone structure. It flows through your cervical vertebra and down along the entire spinal column...so that the bones become pure and clear like a transparent crystal, like a herkimer diamond.

This is how the Crystal energy streams into your arms, bones of the hands, your ribs, breastbone, and pelvic bones...so that these bones find a stable order, as was originally intended and as it is in the universal order. And then it flows through your thighs, knees, and lower leg bones down into the feet.

After the Crystal energy has cleared, cleansed, and stabilized your entire skeleton, it now flows into all the other crystalline structures of your body as well...

And once your entire body is full of this gentle, clarifying, brightening energy, perceive your roots. They reach into the earth from your feet and the base of your spinal column, the coccyx. Let your roots now grow a bit deeper into the earth, into the loving, nourishing core of the earth...

Now take a deep breath and let the nourishing power of the earth—which also allows the crystals and gemstones to grow in their perfect, wonderful forms and colors—flow through you so that you are once again full of power in the here and now.

The Earthangel Tree

Themes
Harmonising cosmic and earthly energy, "connecting heaven and earth," grounding, stability, support.

Description of the Energy
The energy of the Earthangel Tree is encouraging, harmonizing, stabilizing, and calm. It connects the cosmic and earthly energies.

General Tasks
The tree personifies the work of the Earthangel Tree, which is the origin of its name. On the one hand, it roots itself in the earth and finds support and nourishment there. It uses the forces of the earth to grow. On the other hand, it stretches its branches up into the heavens, drinks in the sunlight, and also uses this cosmic energy to grow. As a result, it creates a perfect balance between the forces of heaven and earth.

It also shows that these two forces must be balanced for the earthly body: if its crown stretches up higher than its roots can hold it, it won't be supported and falls over. If its roots are larger than the crown, it can't absorb enough sunlight to grow. Nourished by these energies, the tree grows and develops, blooms, bears fruit, and propagates.

The Earthangel Tree harmonizes the cosmic and earthly energies within every being, according to the needs of the individual. It strengthens our will to live and grow, as well as our powers of self-assertion.

Tasks for Human Beings
The human being is also flooded and nourished by cosmic and earthly energies. We only feel well, have healthy bodies, and can cope successfully with life when the proportions of the two forces

are balanced. The Earthangel Tree supports us in this process. He strengthens and harmonizes the flow of energy, especially the vertical flow of energy.

He also supports an upright, healthy posture. He helps the body to absorb the proper nutrients and fill its own needs so that we can develop and blossom. He connects the aura layers and the chakras with the physical body so that energy and information can flow freely. This leads to liveliness and a desire for action. The energy balance of the body is often improved, allowing cold hands and feet to become warm.

The Earthangel Tree also strengthens our will to live and our initiative. It becomes easier for us to accept our physical body and maintain good health through exercise, sports, and proper nutrition. A feeling of well-being, strength, and trust arises in the body.

Within the body, the Tree energy especially strengthens the back. It allows us to feel where the flow of energy is blocked. It becomes easier to grow into our full size, to occupy our whole body and our entire height. We experience serenity and inner equilibrium, just like a tree that goes through the changes of the seasons year after year, blossoming and bearing fruit at the proper time. The Tree power also supports us in feeling well within our body. If we look at trees or meditate with them, we experience the divine principle of this earthangel. Allow yourself to immerse into their energy and their message.

About This Theme

Some people have difficulties in grounding themselves and keeping their feet on the ground. They make a fragile and delicate impression and frequently have cold hands and feet. They may feel dizzy and have a hard time with "earthly matters." During meditation or energy work, they quickly feel themselves drawn out of their bodies. Yet, they don't like the feeling of being grounded—it feels too narrow, heavy, and tough to them. When they are adequately grounded, they miss the easiness and the sense of flying. It usually takes a while for them to notice the strength and sense of physical well-being created by a balanced flow of energy. But then they also have more joy in life.

In my experience, the phases of grounding and "high-flying" alternate—just like the tree stretches its crown heavenwards in spring and summer, but nourishment and activity take place in the trunk and roots during the winter.

Experiences

Many people feel grounded, stable, calm, balanced, and rooted through the Tree Essence. Some also report that they have a "hearty appetite." The change was quite drastic for me: I had hardly any appetite at all while using the Crystal Essence, but I was ravenous after using the Tree Essence. Above all, I had a desire for "earth products" like potatoes, peanuts, and carrots.

One woman reported that, she calms down and relaxes after a hectic day, when she uses the essence.

Use in the Following Situations
• To harmonize the flow of energy
• To strengthen your will to live and desire for action
• To strengthen your inner stability
• To keep both feet on the ground
• For grounding purposes
• For encouragement
• For aligning the chakras in a vertical manner
• To help plants root and grow

Works together with:
• the complementary Archangel Haniel

Meditation

Relax and connect with your favorite tree (lean on this tree or imagine it in your thoughts or feelings). Become this tree: Feel the trunk that connects the roots and crown...that gives the tree stability, lets it grow upright, and also withstands every storm. Then direct your attention to the roots, how they are rooted in the earth, how deep down they extend, and how they absorb the nourishing energy from the earth...which then flows through the trunk into the crown.

Feel how the branches of the tree extend heavenwards, how they absorb the light of the sun and transform it into usable food. See how they play in the wind and bear blossoms and fruit. Every year, the tree grows , assumes its own proper size, and stretches its roots into the earth and the branches into the sky. Learn from the talents of the tree.

The Earthangel Sun

Themes

Letting the inner light shine, activating the light down to the level of the cells, beauty, joy and cheerfulness, abundance.

Description of the Energy

The energy of the Earthangel Sun is like the sun: warming, loving, calming, cheerful, sunny.

General Tasks

The Earthangel Sun strengthens the radiant beauty within every creation. Just like the sun, it enables everything to shine from within out of the inner abundance. Like the sun, who warms and makes its power available to all, every being is nourished by the overflowing divine force.

All existence can develop the inner beauty and live the principle of overflowing abundance: Flowers exude their fragrance, trees bear much more fruit than they need for their own propagation, and many colors and shades of colors exist. The Earthangel Sun creates the basis for living from abundance and turning this divine aspect into concrete reality.

Tasks for Human Beings

The Earthangel Sun also helps us to find our inner light, the inner sun. He clarifies and brings light into the cells. We become aware, down to the last cell, that we reflect the divine power and beauty, that we are part of God. In the process, we notice where this strength is still lacking in the body—where we are still clinging to old and dark patterns and situations.

The Sun Angel brings the "I am" power into the body. This force expands and intensifies so that we are able to live our true nature from out of the body, so that we can shine and be effective from the basis of our own being. In this way, our bodies can participate in bliss. We develop our natural charisma, an aura that radiates from within our bodies.

The Earthangel Sun brings the sunny aspect into life and lets life become easier since we feel well, comfortable, and cheerful within our bodies.

The energy of the Earthangel Sun strengthens the heart chakra. We can cheerfully rest within ourselves and have an effect on the outside world as a result. Our aura is strengthened, extends its power, and becomes sunnier.

It's clear that we can easily recognize this principle in the radiant power and warmth of the sun. Lay in the sun for a while. Close your eyes and you will comprehend the meaning of this principle.

About This Theme

Instead of my own thoughts, I would like to quote the translation of a poem by E. Kohler that someone once sent me:

The old spring quietly gives
Its water in the same way every day.
I want to be like this spring
And constantly pass on everything within.

But giving, giving—every day
Tell me, spring, isn't this a strain?
As a friend in the yoke, it said to me:
"I am only the spring—and not the source!
It flows to me and I pass it on
This makes my days joyful and glad."

So I live according to the way of the spring
Drawing on strength for life's journey every day
And always want to—happily—pass on
All that the source has given me.

Experiences

During the time that I worked with the energy of the Earthangel Sun, I felt myself to be in high spirits, serene, and cheerful. Life was conspicuously easy and exuberant. Or, in more precise terms, it was my attitude toward life that had changed. There was no longer anything that could easily get me off-center. When I woke up in the morning, there was often a smile on my face.

Other people also told me that they feel happy and cheerful, no longer making life difficult for themselves, through this energy.

Use in the Following Situations
• To find your inner light
• To strengthen the light of your cells
• To find your own center and stay in it
• To relax out of inner strength and abundance
• In situations of depression, heaviness, hopelessness
• When someone is pessimistic
• To improve moods
• To free yourself from emotional entanglements
• For inner well-being
• In situations of emotional need, scarcity, constriction, depression
• Against inner feelings of autumn and winter (November depression/SAD)
• To satisfy inner hunger

Works together with:
• the complementary Archangel Gabriel

Meditation

Sit down in the sun or imagine yourself sitting in the sun. Feel how the sun touches your skin, your face, your hair, your arms, body, and legs. Let yourself be filled by this force so that the warmth and glow of the sun pervade your aura. Let it flow into your muscles, bones, and organs. Feel how this force, which is both animating and calming, penetrates down into each cell.

While you invite the sun's power into your entire body, go to the place within yourself where your inner sun can be found. Look at your sun: How big is it? How close is it? How strong is its illuminating power? Are there clouds or shadows that darken it? What does your inner sun need so that it becomes larger and fills you more completely? What can you do so that the warmth and light of your sun expands more within you and has a stronger effect on your body and every moment of your everyday life?

Allow your inner sun to shine more intensely, as much as is appropriate for you right now.

The Earthangel Fire

Themes

Life force, will to live, vital energy, liveliness, joy in life, inner fire, expansion, striving upward, willpower, growth, penetration, ecstasy, passion, transformation, change.

Description of the Energy

Just like fire, the Earthangel Fire is also powerful, energy-filled, driving, and dynamic.

General Tasks

The Earthangel Fire supports the life force and energy. While the sun represents the calm, continuous, incessantly gentle fire, the element of fire itself is temperamental, enthusing, and provides energy particularly in situations where a great deal of it is needed. The Earthangel Fire represents the powerful will to live. He brings the strength to grow and expand. In every form of being, he strengthens the will for assertion, for assuming the proper place, for wanting to live and reproduce. He is also responsible for transformation, quick renewal, and change.

Tasks for Human Beings

The Earthangel Fire also brings vital energy, the will to live, and joy in life to human beings. With enough inner fire, life becomes a rousing dance. Fire is also the power of expansion. Things that have not yet been clarified or have been concealed up to now, or suppressed, become clarified and transformed.

This earthangel is responsible for the metabolism, the transformation of nutrients into energy, and enables us to apply all of our power. He strengthens the will, and therefore the power of assertion and the ability to lastingly have an effect and make permanent changes. He brings enthusiasm, ebullience, optimism, ambition, self-assurance, courage, confidence, and passion.

People who have too much fire energy are impetuous, impatient, hotheaded, irascible, and aggressive. They tend toward extremes and destructiveness. When people have too little fire energy, they are vulnerable to lethargy, lack of drive, apathy, and boredom. By connecting with the Earthangel Fire, we can harmonize ourselves.

The Earthangel Fire teaches us this divine force in the plants' growth and will to live. Through this example, we can experience and comprehend this principle. But the explosive power of volcanoes and the heat of the lava are also an expression of the divine aspect of Creation.

Experiences

If we have too much fire in us or in situations where we are angry, we should deal with the Fire Essence in a careful and particularly conscious manner. I have the tendency of holding back anger. In a situation where I was angry with Gerhard but pushed it down once again, I tried the Fire Essence to see if the anger would disappear. However, the effect was like pouring gasoline on a fire. The anger boiled over and, contrary to my normal fashion, I yelled at Gerhard and hurled all my pent-up feelings at him. Yet, just as explosively as this fire had come about, it also disappeared in the same way. Within three minutes, it was completely gone and I laughed at myself and the situation. Then everything became peaceful within me.

During the first days that I worked with the Fire Essence, old fears—particularly those related to survival and loss—arose again. Other people reported that their vital force and courage was strengthened by this essence. They were willing to take more risks than before and were successful with them. One therapist observed that this essence strengthened the will to live for people who were seriously ill. They became stronger as a result.

- When you need vital force, courage, and fiery powers of assertion
- To strengthen yourself in new situations
- To gain the courage to start something new
- When you don't have joy and desire in life
- Against a lack of drive and lethargy
- When you want to inspire others
- To strengthen the life force during illness

Works together with:
- the complementary Archangel Michael

Meditation

Your inner wisdom knows very well where your inner fire burns within you. So now let your inner wisdom take you to an inner place where there is enthusiasm, joy in life, willpower, and unbridled strength. Look at your inner fire here. How large is it? How much strength does it have? Does it blaze intensely or is it nearly extinguished? Does it take up a large space or is it just a little fire?

Now also become aware of how much energy you have available for your life. How much enthusiasm do you have for your goals? Do you have the strength to inspire others at this moment? Can you live your life engaged in a passionate dance? How does this inner fire shape your life?

Now invite the Earthangel Fire and ask him to form your inner fire in the way that is best for you at the moment. Ask him to give your inner fire the ability of adapting itself to situations: If you need a great deal of fire, it should expand; if you need less fire, it should condense itself into the right size. Also let him shape the fire in each individual cell so that you have an optimal metabolism that functions harmoniously.

And while the Fire Angel shapes your inner fire to your best advantage, observe what happens and perceive what changes there are in your feelings, thoughts, or your entire life. As the Fire Angel creates an optimal condition for you, take leave from him and return to the outer world, into the here and now.

The Earthangel Water

Feeling, flowing, movement, reaching the goal, adapting, being in the moment

Description of the Energy

The energy of the Earthangel Water is soft, flowing devoted, adaptable, harmonizing, yet clear and determined. Nothing stops it from reaching its goal, even if detours are necessary.

General Tasks

The largest percentage of the earth's surface consists of the element of water. The same applies to the human body. Consequently, the Earthangel Water is also a very important principle for the earth. His power maintains the flow of life, of change, and of movement. He teaches how to adapt and change form, yet still not be lost. He is the constant flow of everything within the eternal cycle of change. All things change, nothing remains as it is, and yet the core of being remains the same.

No other element can so easily change its form, switching back and forth from one aggregate state to another. So the Earthangel Water brings all created beings the strength to adapt to their living space, to the circumstances around them, and still develop the form within them. He supports the power of reaching the goal, no matter if this goal is growth, expansion, a place, or a form. Information can also be absorbed and transmitted just as easily.

Tasks for Human Beings

Just as the water that flows in nature appears in different degrees of liveliness and various forms—the bubbling spring, the raging stream, the broad river, the wild ocean, the placid lake, the pond, the rain, the fog, the clouds, the ice—and still remains water, the Earthangel Water also strengthens our ability of adapting to a great variety of situations without losing our basic nature. We learn to be in the here and now and attuned to the present moment.

If something completely different occurs in the next moment, we can flow along, tackling blocks and resistance until we have hollowed out a path through them. Until then, we flow around them. This earthangel teaches us the power of not letting anything stop us when we want to reach a goal. He makes it possible for us to achieve a goal without fighting, solely through endurance and steadfastness.

This earthangel also brings the principle of flowing into the body: Everything that is congested—no matter whether feelings, tears, or fluids—is opened. Flowing and letting things flow is the natural state of being. It is just as natural as liveliness and joy, as constant movement and renewal.

Our body is changing constantly: Cells die off every day and new ones are formed, and yet our basic nature remains the same. This principle teaches us to be in motion and easily set ourselves in motion, to flow but still essentially remain stable.

Water is feeling and so this earthangel also teaches us to deal with our feelings, especially when they are expressed on the physical level. He harmonizes and stabilizes the emotional aura. In the process, what has been held in the depths may rise to the surface. He teaches how to be empathetic, how to become one with others, as well as setting boundaries and maintaining our own form.

Just like water, we also learn to dissolve and absorb so that we can easily let go of things and give away what we have absorbed afterward. This is also helpful when doing therapeutic work.

The Earthangel Water teaches us his principle in the flowing and circulation of water. At streams and seas, at springs and lakes, in the rain, fog, and haze we experience and comprehend this divine principle.

Experiences

The power of this earthangel makes everything soft and flowing. Some users felt an inner harmony and learned to adapt without losing themselves in the process. Others had the feeling of losing the ground beneath their feet. The fear of losing control, the fear of what happens when the rigidity and tension is released, also arose. In the same respect, the places in the body that are tensed and cramped also clearly reveal themselves.

Use in the Following Situations

- To start being in the moment and agreeing with the moment
- To relieve tension and hardening
- To get things flowing, to let suppressed feelings and tears flow
- To learn devotion
- To let go at the right moment
- For detoxification and clearing
- To let energies absorbed from other people flow on
- To adapt without losing yourself
- Helps when you tend toward extremes
- To find the easiest path to the goal, also applies to work
- To trust that you can reach the goal, even if you don't yet know the way
- For cheerfulness, joy, playfulness
- Together with the archangel Raphael and Kwan Yin, this force supports the work with feelings

Works together with:

- the complementary Archangel Raphael

Meditation

While you observe your breath, how it flows into your lungs and back out again so your chest rises and falls, let yourself be rocked on the arms of the Earthangel Water. Like a gentle rocking on the waves, you are lightly moved while you have a sense of safeness and security. He lovingly rocks you in his arms and invites you to a journey, a journey through the world of his element. This is a journey through the principle of water, the principle of change and constancy.

And while you feel safe and secure, like a child in the mother's womb, softly surrounded by nourishing and invigorating water, you turn into water yourself, into water bubbling from a spring. This water continuously and ceaselessly gushes from the inside of the earth. Nothing can stand in its way, and nothing can stop it. The power always finds a way, pushes on to the outside and flows in its own path from there.

You flow from wherever you start, are fed by the continuously flowing supply of the spring, unite with other streams and become stronger and wider. You bubble and hiss across the rocks, you pour yourself over the edges of rocks into deep lakes. You become a calm lake and the sun and moon are reflected on your surface....It is dark and silent, timeless, in the depths of the lake...

Yet, you do not stay here. At some point you leave the lake, drawn by the current that moves toward the sea. You flow past obstacles, unceasingly, time and again, and at some point, these obstacles will no longer be there. The obstacles will lose their edges and corners through the constantly flowing force of the water, without the water intending this to happen and without costing any of its strength. And so you continue to flow, become a wide river that rolls through various landscapes, sometimes flooding its banks or moving leisurely in its bed.

You always strive for your goal without knowing what the goal is and yet achieve it, uniting with the sea, the sea with its constant up and down motions, with the waves that roll gently and easily onto the shore, back and forth...Or you hit against the rocks surging and storming, spraying with the surf. Time and again the sea spray hisses and foams as it falls back into the sea to soon churn up again and burst into thousands of drops. With unbelievable strength, you storm and rush against the cliffs of the shore, rear up to a height of many feet, and then smash onto the hard stone, which you form and change, steadfastly and continuously, without even wanting to form or change it.

Whatever happens occurs in the eternal flow of change. You sink back into the depths of the sea in order to once again rise up. Or you are carried by the force of the sun, one drop that becomes increasingly lighter and rises, that dissolves in the air and becomes lighter, that expands and turns into a gas, yet still remains water. It floats and unites with other drops of water. You gather into a mass, but this time into light piles of clouds, enormous structures that float easily above the earth. You immerse yourself, collect yourself, unite with the others, and flow. This is an eternal cycle, a constant state of change, a continual flowing, and yet everything remains the same.

And then you feel how the arms of the angel gently rock you back and forth, the angel that teaches you this principle. Now it carries you back into the real world of your human body, in which water is an essential component. And while you begin to move your body, you may perhaps be surprised that you carry this power within you, yet it is compact and steadfast—clear and awake, powerful and lively.

The Earthangel Earth

Themes
Stability, patience, concentration, endurance, being nourished, giving structure

Description of the Energy
The energy of the Earthangel Earth is nourishing, calm, cautious (some people would call it tough), powerful like an elephant, cheerful, and serene. It imparts the feeling of standing with both feet on the ground and being supported.

General Tasks
The Earthangel Earth completes the materialization. His concentrating, unifying force condenses and solidifies energy and vibration, whereby solid matter is created. He is the preserver, the nourisher, and conveys the sense of the right point in time and of stability.

Tasks for Human Beings
The energy of the Earthangel Earth nourishes, strengthens, and also grounds human beings. It connects us with the qualities that the element earth also represents: stability, serenity, patience, strength, richness, and abundance. People notice this strength and stability in their bodies, which they may also experience as heaviness or tenacity. Those with predominating air qualities, who are usually "flighty and fluctuating", have a particularly hard time with this force. They may clearly feel resistance against the sense of being grounded, of stability and "walking the path step-by-step." This resistance can be resolved through positive experiences. The ability of waiting and not acting too quickly is strengthened. These individuals receive the feeling for the right point in time and the impulse appears to come from within. "Timing is important" is what the angel appears to teach us.

Tolerance arises from the feeling of wealth. Everything can grow and order is certain to result. The energy of this angel helps us to materialize visions and ideal realities. The natural cycle of becoming and dying is recognized and accepted. Tolerance develops, even toward change.

With the Earthangel Earth, change does not occur in the same way as with Air or Water. It is a slow, unhurried opening to a new structure, a new form. It almost appears as if we are clinging to the old, but change does occur on the basis of deliberation and thorough examination. And therefore remains considerably more stable than changes that result through the Earthangels Air and Water.

This energy also strengthens the connection between the subtle and the physical bodies, as well as their unity, especially when the subtle plane resonates at a much higher level than the physical level. As a result, the body can form a stabile foundation for the increase in subtle vibrations. It compensates for fluctuations. This means that the vibrational frequency increases in a continuous manner, at the right point in time, and develops in a "healthy" way, without throwing the energy system out of balance. Through the energy of this angel, the stability of the subtle regions is also increased, but without solidifying them.

We sense this divine aspect of the Creation in the beauty of the mountains, hills, and valleys, in the caves and in the ground that bears everything. We also sense it in the flow of the hot lava and in its cooled form.

About This Theme

Particularly in times when the subtle aura resonates at an extremely high level and there is an enormous discrepancy between the solid body and the aura, the energy of this angel has a special significance. Through meditation, special techniques, and the general changes in energy on the earth, the vibrations of the subtle bodies can shift very quickly. Extreme physical and emotional reactions, which can be very unpleasant, may occur.

The energy of the Earthangel Earth connects these two levels so that they can only resonate on a higher level together. As a result, the discrepancy and tension does not rise as much. The picture of a fast horse and a wagon illustrate this condition. If the horse isn't adequately connected to the wagon, it bolts when it receives an energy impulse and runs away. The connection with the wagon is broken. However, if the horse is firmly connected to the wagon, it pulls the wagon with it when there is an energy impulse. Although it doesn't move as quickly as without it, the wagon does not remain behind. Both move forward together and remain connected.

Some people are afraid of opening up to the principle of earth—the solidity, stability, and the themes of material, money, possessions, and status—because they fear losing their freedom and flexibility. Possessions, which simultaneous also mean grounding, bring obligations and dependence with them.

How often have we encountered the attitude of "it is easier for a camel to go through the eye of a needle than for a rich man to enter the kingdom of God" on the spiritual path? So we prefer to stay poor, ascetic, and flexible. Yet, avoidance does not mean that the theme has been resolved. Especially not when the desire for luxury and prosperity slumbers hidden in our unconscious minds.

Experiences

Through the energy of this earthangel, people have experienced how they became calm and serene. Many felt grounded and connected to the earth. This is especially true in situations where their bodies were not firmly connected with their subtle aura and they didn't feel like they were even in their bodies. They also felt strengthened in crisis situations. However, there were other individuals who did not like this energy at all. They became aware of their own extreme resistance against life on this earth.

Use in the Following Situations
- When you feel airy, fluttery, or lacking in concentration
- When you want to connect with your inner stability
- For grounding (can also be experienced as too vehement)
- To feel the easiness and joy of the earth
- For connecting subtle and physical bodies
- To stabilize and strengthen the subtle body
- To stabilize the physical body, without it becoming inflexible
- To reconnect with the stable, powerful physical form
- To come to rest
- Against difficulties in everyday life or with routines
- To make peace with the earth and life on earth
- To accept the cycle of life, becoming and dying
- Can also have a clarifying effect on resistance to the theme of money, possessions, success, and strength (however, also to illustrate the resistance and make it conscious)

Works together with:
- the complementary Archangel Uriel

Meditation

Imagine that you are lying in a meadow, in the pleasant sunlight, surrounded by plants that make you feel good. You breathe in the pure, clear air and it appears to cleanse your lungs and your entire body. While you listen to the song of the birds and the rustling of the leaves in the wind, you feel beneath your body the earth that supports you.

*While you close your eyes, or have already closed them, you appear to be slowly and securely carried off into the realm of the earth. Safe in the powerful, loving hands of an angel, you are well protected as you slowly sink into the realm of the pleasant, velvety darkness and the clear, pure air continues to stream into your lungs because the realm of earth is filled with air. The earth is stable and so you **slowly** sink deeper.*

You are supported and nourished...and absorb the quality of the earth into yourself. You sense and recognize which qualities are good for you and what you can learn from the earth realm...Allow yourself to sink as deeply as is right for you...And perhaps you are being carried into the various layers since the earth bears many forms within itself: the pliant and soft...the crystalline and stable.

Deep inside itself, the earth is hot and liquid. This is the primeval force from which the nourishing surface has been formed. The primeval force that contains everything found on the surface. The primeval force from which the earth can continuously form itself anew. And this primeval force sometimes pushes its way to the outside to reform the surface of the earth in these places.

Now allow yourself to slowly detach from the nourishing earth force and the earthangel slowly and safely carries you back to the top. And while you once again breathe in the fresh, pure air of the meadow, you listen to the song of the birds and the rustling of the wind. As the sun touches your skin, perceive how this journey has nourished and strengthened you, how you have become increasingly awake and alive, being back in the here and now. You stretch and feel the desire to express your strength.

The Earthangel Air

Themes

Flexibility, change, easiness, exchange, freedom, independence, clarity and power of thoughts, intuition, communication.

Description of the Energy

The Earthangel Air is nourishment and movement. Almost all forms of life on earth need air to live. However, in contrast to the nourishment of the angel Earth, Air is light and flexible. This nourishment strengthens the flexible, lively, flowing vital force and energy. The Air angel carries divine vital energy like *prana* and all the other forms.

Air is quickly exchanged since it is light and flexible. So information flows over the continents. The air carries dust, water, seeds, and animals over great distances. The Earthangel Air is also an angel of communication and exchange.

Tasks for Human Beings

The Earthangel Air teaches us to make it easy for ourselves and not take life on earth, our feelings, and situations too seriously. Quickly and flexibly, we can move from one situation to the next, changing from one place to another without getting stuck or clinging. And like a gentle breeze can become a raging storm within a short period of time, we can also change our moods, attitudes, and feelings at every moment.

The Air angel teaches us to "be in the moment" and enjoy every instant. The Air angel clears and strengthens the mental area, the thoughts and the power of the mind. Mental information can then flow unimpeded through the entire body. As quick as the wind, we can grasp correlations and drive away the obscuring clouds. However, the mental area includes not only the rational mind. This earthangel also strengthens our intuition and powers of discernment. The Earthangel Air also teaches through exchange and communication.

Immerse yourself in this divine principle by observing the wind, the stillness of the air, and the violence of a storm that once again subsides as if nothing had happened and leaves a deep silence behind.

Experiences

People who work with this force report that their mental powers are strengthened. They have often been astonished to discover how clearly they comprehend correlations and how quickly they can react and make decisions. And they also succeed in more easily switching off their minds, leaving thoughts from other situations behind them, and being in the here and now.

Use in the Following Situations
- To be in the present moment
- For strengthening your intuition
- For clearing the third eye
- Against ponderous thinking
- When you get stuck in pessimistic thoughts and worries
- To get over negative moods and emotions
- When life appears to be overwhelming you
- For people who live in seclusion and have retreated into their shell because they take life too seriously
- For people who have difficulties in moving, who cling to the material world and the earth
- When you have problems with relaxing or changing situations
- For better communication

Works together with:
- the complementary Archangel Chamuel

Meditation

Observe your breathing for a while. Observe how you inhale and exhale. With every inhalation, absorb the power and liveliness of the air into yourself. With every exhalation, let go of whatever is old and used up. *Allow as many of the heavy things to leave you as is right for you at the moment. Allow heaviness, worries, and unnecessary thoughts to vanish more and more with every breath—and observe how your body becomes increasingly lighter and freer as a result.*

Now allow your breath and the Earthangel Air to carry you through your entire body. Like a leaf sailing on the soft breeze, the angel carries you into your lungs—which become stronger and take in pure, clear air and energy. It carries you through your neck. Whatever is stuck there can now be released. It carries you through your head—which is cleared and cleansed, down through the spinal column—where the angel clears the channels and strengthens the nerve connections, and expands throughout your entire back—cleansing and regenerating it.

The Air angel also flies through the stomach area. Your belly rises, sometimes more gently and sometimes more vigorously, according to how much energy and strength you need to regulate and stabilize your inner digestive processes—and also through all the organs of the abdominal and chest area. Then the energy flows into your arms, which are almost as light and movable as the air—and finally into your legs as it cleanses and clears them.

While the energy and the air flow through your body, clearing, cleansing, and nourishing it, allow yourself to become familiar with the various powers of the air. Sometimes you breathe gently and lightly, as velvety as a baby. It almost appears that you don't need any air, you are so deeply relaxed...And then there are phases in which you breathe intensively, such as during sports or when you exert yourself. Then you are full of vital energy and liveliness. Experience the difference...And then calm your breathing once again and find the rhythm and intensity that makes you lively and harmonious.

Now let the Earthangel Air gently bring you back into the here and now so that you can enjoy your liveliness and strength.

LightBeings Archangel and Earthangel Essences

The LightBeings Archangel and Earthangel Essences contain the energetic vibrations of the archangels and earthangels bound to a carrier substance—usually a water/alcohol mixture. Through this carrier substance, the energy is transmitted to the physical energy system of human beings, as well as to animals and plants, rooms and places. The essences harmonize whatever is disharmonious and balance what has lost its equilibrium. They clear and dissolve energetic blocks and strengthen the power in our own system. They orient us toward our highest potential and support the development of the abilities that we bear within us. This is how they stabilize the equilibrium of body, mind, and soul. Through their own vibration, they work on a non-material level.

All LightBeings essences serve the process of becoming conscious, of personal development and spiritual growth. They are well-tested, efficient tools on the path to a fulfilled life. With them, our next steps can be recognized and taken more easily and quickly. If you would like to know more about the effects of the subtle LightBeings Essences, I recommend our *LightBeings Master Essences* book. In addition, it contains a comprehensive and easily understandable basic section on the effects of energetic remedies, the correlation between illness and vibration, the human energy system, and how information can have an effect on human beings.

How the LightBeings Archangel and Earthangel Essences Came to Us

The LightBeings Archangel and Earthangel Essences are a gift from the spiritual world, a gift from the angels to humanity. In November of 1997, we received the message that it was time for us to make the Archangel Essences. Up to that time, we had only worked with the Ascended Master energies.

At first, we refused to do this since it meant even more work, new bottles, and more space—and our house was already bursting at the seams. But then it quickly became clear to us that the work with the archangels was the next step in our development. The Ascended Master Essences had already accompanied us for a long time and we had taken enormous steps with them—we were sometimes astonished at everything that happened and how easily and quickly we left the old behind us.

But now we were meant to enter a new level. We very quickly discovered that the energies of the archangels have a different effect than those of the masters. The master essences involved transformation work, working through things, and digesting them little by little. But the work with the archangels happened in leaps and bounds. We soon received the message from the spiritual world that these essences were associated with perceiving and surrendering.

And so the next adventure of development began for us. As with the master essences, we first made an essence for ourselves and worked with it intensively for about one month. During this time, we experienced the energy and effect of the respective archangel, cleared our energy system, and attuned ourselves to this source of energy. We had quite consciously avoided reading anything about the energy of the archangels beforehand so that their power could have an effect on us without any outside influences. This allowed us to immerse ourselves in the energy and experience it without any bias.

The essences that we made for ourselves had a different effect than those that we distribute today. I sometimes lovingly called them "scouring essences" because they allowed us to completely attune ourselves to the energy of the respective archangel, dissolving our blocks on this theme.

During the work with the archangels, I noticed something else: I had loved the masters, but I felt completely at home with the archangels. And so I was very thankful that we had received and accepted this assignment.

In October of 1998, while we were in the middle of the process with the archangels, the name "earthangel" came up for the first time. We hardly knew what to do with it at first, but then it became clear to us: There would be a third group of essences that come from the earthangels and have a greater effect on the material realm.

As much as I felt at home with the archangels, I was uneasy about the idea of the earthangels. I had never liked to be involved with earthly things and had always rejected the idea of making elf, deva, or elemental essences. And, as always, the resistance showed me: "This is your next step."

When we began with the third group of essences, I quickly felt the pleasant effect on my body. Today I am happy that the Earthangel Essences are available to me on my path and I love these energies just as much as those of the ascended masters.

Our system, which now includes three levels, is complete:

THE ARCHANGEL ESSENCES

Perceiving   They remind us of our divine nature and remove the veils that darken it.

THE MASTER ESSENCES

Understanding They help us live our true being in daily life. Since the ascended masters have lived on the earth themselves, in contrast to the angels they recognize the difficulties, stumbling blocks, and entanglements in which we get stuck time and again. These make it difficult for us to live our true being in everyday life.

THE EARTHANGEL ESSENCES

Integrating The essences of the earthangels support the body so that it more easily adapts to the higher vibrations and integrates them. They harmonize and stabilize the connection between the subtle and the physical bodies and help us to manifest the abilities and characteristics that we have brought with us into this world. The elements angels and the Element-Balance Spray can also be used for the balancing of rooms and Feng Shui purposes.

The various essences also work on different levels of the body and the energy system. The Earthangel Essences regulate the physical level, the denser subtle aura, and the patterns and knowledge stored in the body. The Master Essences essentially harmonize the aura, the energy channels, and the chakras, while the Archangel Essences primarily work on the spiritual aura body and the higher chakras. After a person uses the essences for a while, the effect also extends to the other areas.

These essences are available on the three levels:
9 Archangel Essences (Uriel, Haniel, Michael, Gabriel, Chamuel, Raphael, Jophiel, Zadkiel, and Metatron)
21 Master Essences (Maha Chohan, Lao Tse, El Morya, Kwan Yin, Christ, Djwal Khul, Sanat Kumara, Angelica, Orion, Kamakura, Kuthumi, Lady Nada, Serapis Bey, Victory, Saint Germain, Hilarion, Pallas Athene, Lady Portia, Helion, Aeolus, and Mary)
7 Earthangel Essences (Crystal, Sun, Tree, Earth, Fire, Water, and Air)

3 mixtures (Relax for Crisis Situations, Travel, and Element-Balance Spray).

Mixtures of all the three levels have proved to be especially effective: one Archangel, one Master, and one Integration Essence each are selected, mixed, and applied like one individual essence (also see Application). As a result, the next theme will be worked on simultaneously on all three levels. Everyone who works in this way confirms that mixing the essence has both the most powerful and the most harmonious effect.

How Can I Select the Appropriate Essence?

There are no wrong essences. As you can see from the description of the angel energies, there is a theme behind each force that we should develop or desire to develop. We already have it in our "backpack," but haven't unpacked it yet or haven't unpacked it completely. However, there are themes that we already master quite well—and when we use an essence for them, we will probably not notice any kind of major change. Then it just fine-tunes them. We have more difficulties with other themes—and the appropriate essence for them can bring up old forms of resistance, make us aware of them, and effect quite a few changes.

The essences are meant to be supportive for our growth steps and should therefore be selected according to the pending theme in life. You can generally ask: "What essences support me in a pleasant way for the next step? However, you can also ask for guidance in a certain situation (such as an upcoming conversation, a meeting, on a specific theme (like a relationship or your job), or in the development of abilities (such as intuition, decision-making power, or clairvoyance).

For many people, there is a difference in whether they ask for "the appropriate essence" or for "the appropriate essence that

supports me in a pleasant way." In the latter case, they unconsciously give themselves the permission for things to also occur
gently. But if their pattern is "only when things are difficult or
I suffer does much happen," their subconscious mind will always choose the essence that takes the harder path.

There are several possibilities for selecting the best essence:

According to the theme
Since you are working on life themes and soul qualities, you
can take the list of essences and see what appeals to you. This
method has the disadvantage of the "blind spot." We avoid
selecting the themes that we do not want to see, even though
they are appropriate. In addition, it may be that an integrating
or resolving step must be taken before the actual theme can be
approached. We may also overlook this when making a direct
choice.

By drawing a card
There are energized selection cards available for the essences.
Similar to the Tarot, you can use the cards to find the upcoming
theme and the appropriate essence. To do this, you should
consciously formulate the question in your mind since it does
make a difference whether you are asking about the upcoming
theme or for support in a certain situation, or about the theme
of your entire life. The cards are also an excellent "diagnostic
tool" to find out which theme is behind specific situations.

Ask your question (for example: Which essence will support
me at the moment in a pleasant way?) and then draw a card. If
you want to create a mixture, then sort the cards in three piles:
the Archangel Essences, the Master Essences, and the Earthangel
Essences. Then draw one card from each pile (also see Mixtures,
page 178). Your higher self and subconscious mind will direct
your hand—the rational mind will doubt and ask the question:
"But couldn't it also be another card?" This is normal. Decide
and take the card that you have selected.

Testing methods
Other test methods like the pendulum, biotensor, electro-acupuncture according to Voll, and the kinesiological muscle test are suitable selection methods.

Intuition
You can also let yourself be directly guided by your intuition.

Application

The carrier substance for the energy is a water/alcohol mixture. You can apply a few drops of this mixture to areas of the body. Another method is fanning or spraying them into the aura and chakras. The tincture or with the dripper can also be put into your mouth. Let yourself be guided by your intuition when deciding how to apply the different essence forms. A good time for using the essences is in the morning after getting up and evenings before going to bed.

You should work with an essence for a longer period of time (at least two weeks) so that the blocks can be resolved on a deep level. When this has been completed, one level of the theme is often integrated. However, since we usually go through the theme a number of times, the essence will most likely appear again. When I have completed a theme for now, I forget to take the essence. At the beginning, I take it several times a day. But later, I use it less and less.

Moreover, the essences are suitable for energizing rooms, to create a harmonious atmosphere, and as a bath additive.

Selecting the Essences for Others

You can also select essences for others. We recommend that you use the selection cards for this purpose. Attune yourself to the other person by visualizing a connecting light between your hearts, for example. Then draw a card with the question: "What is the appropriate essence that would support name in a pleasant way?"

The essences can be used for children and also for animals. We have already received an abundance of positive feedback in this regard. Make the selection in the same way as described in the "Selecting the Essences for Others" sections.

Mixtures

As we have already said: You can make your own essence mixtures. To do so, select the appropriate components. One method of doing this is dividing the card set into the three areas of Archangel Essences, Master Essences, and Earthangel Essences. Draw one card from each pile. Take an empty bottle, put equal parts of each respective essence into the bottle, and then shake it a number of times. It's important to shake it because the individual essences are then mixed into a new essence. The mixtures have a different effect than if you would use the individual essences one after the other.

Mixtures can be made for the upcoming period of time, for a particular situation, or for a specific theme. Making a *birthday mixture* for yourself or others is a good idea. It should contain the three essences that will provide support in the coming year of life. There have been some very positive experiences with these mixtures—and they are a special gift.

For frequent themes we offer some ready-made mixtures:

Travel Essence

The Travel Essence is a mixture of Uriel, Tree, and Serapis Bey. When traveling, I have greatly appreciated its effects: I no longer have jet lag on long flights. Jet lag occurs because the aura bodies are torn by the high speed and need some time to become integrated again. Especially people with high vibrations, whose connection between the physical body and the aura is not very stable, suffer from this phenomenon. They feel dizzy, lacking in orientation, and unwell. This can also occur when traveling by train or car.

The Travel Mixture strengthens the connection between the physical and subtle body, as well as stabilizing the aura. This makes it easier for the aura to remain connected with the body during the journey. When traveling across time zones, also place a drop of Kamakura Essence on the third eye. This will quickly reset your biological clock to the local time.

The Travel Essence also helps during inner journeys. It stabilizes an individual and makes it easier to return. This essence is also helpful when you have a difficult time freeing yourself from dreams after you get up in the morning or being totally in the present moment.

Element-Balance Spray

The Element-Balance Spray is a mixture of Fire, Water, Earth, Air, and Tree. This essence has an outstanding effect on the harmonization of the elemental powers in the body and in rooms. Since it balances the forces, it is also very suitable for Feng Shui. I have had good experiences with this spray in computer workplaces. When computers run for longer period of time, the vibrations change. When this spray is used, the area once again feels harmonized and rich in energy.

The Element-Balance Spray has a harmonizing effect on bad moods. It is the complementary earthangel energy for the Archangel Zadkiel.

Combination with Other Techniques

The essences can be combined with other techniques like homeopathy, rebalancing, kinesiology, reflex massage, flower essences, and so forth. The effect of the LightBeings Essences begins in an individual's spiritual realm. From there, the effect extends to the other levels. Through the combination with other techniques, we become aware of the next learning step and energetic blocks dissolve more quickly. Changes are more easily integrated into everyday life. Some therapists give their clients an individual essence mixture after the treatment session as "homework." They report that the therapy success is better stabilized as a result.

How the Essences Are Made

The essences are made in a meditative state and completed in a number of steps. Since we have received the attunement with the forces or initiation into them, we can connect with the energy source at any time. After the preparations, we ask the beings to put their energy *directly* into the prepared carrier substances. The energy does not flow through us and is also not a form of mental energizing.

After the carrier substance is energized, its energy is sealed so that it does not fade away absorb any foreign vibrations from the outside. Then the energized substance is filled into the bottles and the bottles have their energy sealed as well. During the production of the essences, there is no shaking, diluting, or potentiating. Each essence that you receive has been directly energized and is just as clear and powerful as it was when it was energized.

Living Angelic Lightness on Earth

At my seminars and lectures, I repeatedly encounter people who are surrounded by an angelic charisma and easiness. However, they do not feel this way about themselves. They think that life is difficult and hard, tough and full of problems. They have the feeling that they made a mistake in coming to the earth and want to go back home again. I personally am quite familiar with this feeling.

Yet, I have always had this certainty inside myself: Life is easy. But I experienced the opposite in the outside world. And so I had the tendency to quickly resign and wish I were somewhere else. But then this image came to me:

The unborn "souls of easiness", some of them are also angels, are looking at life on earth from the "in-between region." All of them want to go to the earth and immerse themselves in the adventure of feelings by letting themselves be shaken to the core. And so they look at the life of human beings and puzzle about why people do not recognize that it is easy. They do not understand why people in the body so readily let themselves be captured by their emotions. Above all, they do not understand why the people do not recognize this themselves. Some of these souls have personally experienced the heaviness and entanglements of life on earth. But most of the souls on earth have experienced this as well, yet they still fall into entanglements and dramas over and over again.

Suddenly, the "souls of easiness" see the age around the millennium. It is a time of change, an era in which much happens here on the earth. It is a time in which many human beings will take the path of consciousness and awaken. "This is where we want to be. We want to contribute our easiness. We will show the others how to live lightly and cheerfully on the earth" they call out enthusiastically and throw themselves into the excitement of incarnation. Some angels also participate in this experience.

And then the souls immerse themselves in the density of the earth, feel the heaviness of the body, and grow into the film of life. Like someone at the movies, they are fascinated by the images that run in front of their eyes, get caught up in the intensive feelings, and overpowered by the burden and weight of the earth. They think that the illusion of the film is reality. They forget their enthusiasm for their assignment. The memory of easiness slumbers weakly within them, yet this memory must be from another time since everything is difficult here on the earth. Until they remember and begin the game—the game of finding out how human beings can live easily and happily in the density of the material world.

Conclusion

Angels accompany us—so that we can experience the divine force within us. As you now know, angels do not want us to remain "small" and always just need their help to solve problems. They want us to develop the beauty and power within us that they have never lost. Full of love and acceptance, they are glad to help us time and again, without any limitations, on this path. They help us discover the qualities that they represent without ourselves—and then to develop and live them. In this way, our lives can become an easy, fulfilled, and cherished adventure. It begins to be fun, and we can increasingly laugh about the drama that we create for ourselves and the difficulties that we get bogged down in. And with our laughter, with our joy, a new chapter also begins for the angels: Instead of helping us out of the entanglements, they can then accompany us to even greater fulfillment and bliss—to the life that we love without limitation.

Bibliography

1   Bandini, Pietro. *Drachenwelt* Stuttgart-Vienna-Bern: Weitbrecht Verlag, 1996.

   The Holy Bible, Revised Standard Version. New York: Harper & Brothers, 1952.

2   Die Brücke zur Freiheit (editor): *Engel—unsere hilfreichen Freunde, Berlin.*

3   Divyanand, Soami. *Engel—Elemente und Energien.* In: *Religionen im Gespräch, Engel—Elemente und Energien,* vol. 2, Balve, 1992, pg. 304ff.

4   Divyanand, Soami (2). *Nicht perfekt sein wollen.* In: *Visionen* 4/99, Herrischried: Sandila Verlag, pg. 17-19.

5   Fox, Matthew & Sheldrake, Rupert. *The Physics of Angels. A Realm Where Spirit and Science Meet.* San Francisco: Harper, 1996.

6   Heinz, Sabine. Information supplied via telephone. Writer of *Symbole der Kelten.* Darmstadt: Schirner Verlag, 1998.

7   Magonet, Jonathan. *Ein wenig niedriger als die Engel.* In: *Religionen im Gespräch, Engel—Elemente und Energien,* vol. 2, Balve, 1992, pg. 269ff.

8   Marooney, Kimberly. *Angel Blessings.* Carmel, CA: Merrill-West Publishing, 1995.

9   Schimmel, Annemarie. *Engel im Islam.* In: in *Religionen im Gespräch, Engel—Elemente und Energien,* vol. 2, Balve, 1992, pg. 282ff.

10 Schneider, Petra & Pieroth, Gerhard K., *LightBeings—Master Essences.* Twin Lakes/WI: Arcana Publishing, 1998.

11 Schneider, Petra & Pieroth, Gerhard K., *Hilfe aus der geistigen Welt.* Aitrang: Windpferd Verlag, 1999.

12 Schwarzenau, Paul. *Die himmlischen Hierarchien des Areopagita und die Engellehre von Rudolph Steiner.* In: *Religionen*

im Gespräch, Engel—Elemente und Energien, vol. 2, Balve, 1992, pg. 197ff.

13 Seul, Winfried. *Engel und Daemonen, Biblisches Weltbild und heutige Zugaenge.* St. Augustin: Thesis. 1993.

14 Wenberg, Egon. *Ein Plädoyer für Engel.* Freiburg: Bauer-Verlag, 1994.

Gerhard K. Pieroth und Petra Schneider

The Authors

Dr. Petra Schneider, born in 1960, studied and received her doctor's degree in the subject of agronomy at the University of Bonn. In 1990, she completed additional training for the teaching profession, administrative work, and consultation and accepted a position as an official at the Agricultural Chamber. There she dealt with questions related to environmental protection in agriculture and the topics of brown coal and village development.

During this time she became intensely interested in the meaning of her life. As a result, she realized that her professional activities didn't provide fulfillment for her life. She quit the secure, life-long position and began a deep involvement with subtle energies, meditation, and the possibilities of holistic development of the self. Among other things, one aspect of this was training to become a Reiki teacher, NLP practitioner, and meditation teacher.

She now works as a holistic personal counselor and gives seminars.

Since 1994 she has been intensely involved with the energies of the Ascended Masters, resulting in the creation of the LightBeings Master Essences.

Gerhard K. Pieroth, born in 1956, is a certified industrial engineer and worked as an employee of the computer manufacturer IBM in the production, marketing, and sales departments. As a secondary occupation, he was a lecturer at several institutes of higher learning.

In 1988, the failure of his marriage and collapse of his world view lead him on the search for meaning in his life and brought his first experiences with meditation. He opened up increasingly to the abilities he hadn't lived out before that point and quit his job in 1992. Then he trained to be a Reiki teacher and NLP practitioner, among other things. Parallel to this, he trained in the field of adult education and currently works as a holistic success and management consultant, as well as a coach and trainer at companies and for individuals.

Together with Petra, he produces the LightBeings Master Essences and holds seminars.

Expression of Thanks

To my soul sister and friend Shantidevi Felgenhauer. She guided me in a loving way on the inner journeys to forgotten portions of my soul. Together we have explored the various levels and energies of the spiritual world. Our many conversations brought clarity, and she provided important impulses for this book.

Many thanks to Karen Crane for her loving and kind support of our project and for her friendship. It's a pleasure for us to work together with her.

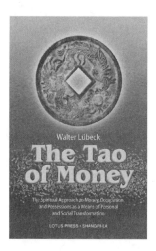

Walter Lübeck

The Tao of Money

The Spiritual Approach to Money, Occupation, and Possessions as a Means of Personal and Social Transformation

The Tao of Money explores how to heal material consciousness. For author Walter Lübeck, money can be equated with energy, something that manifests itself in every conceivable manner. This fascinating book about money contains many exercises on its spiritual meaning, work, occupation, and much more. How you treat money in your everyday life also expresses the inner state of your soul.

To a large extent, money has a deep spiritual dimension: Money activates the root chakra, wealth sets the love-of-life chakra into motion, and work affects the power chakra and the heart chakra. You can awaken the expression chakra through your job and use possessions to increase your kundalini energy. Discover what type of money person you are.

160 pages · $14.95
ISBN 0-914955-62-4
(Lotus Press · Shangri-La)

Petra Schneider/Gerhard Pieroth

LightBeings

Master Essences · A Path to Mastering Life · A Systematic Handbook to the Energy of the Ascended Masters

This book systematically introduces the LightBeings Master Essences, which contain the energetic vibration of the "Ascended Masters" and help dissolve mental, emotional, physical, and spiritual blocks. This book offers a path to mastery in life, which means growing beyond personal limitations and becoming more conscious. The LightBeings Master Essences have an effect on the mental, emotional, physical, and spiritual level. They also help dissolve the blocks that we have. The result is that we acquire the courage to take action, to trust and be joyful.

272 pages · $16.95
ISBN 0-910261-18-0
(ARCANA Publishing)

Herbs and other natural health products and information are often available at natural food stores or metaphysical bookstores. If you cannot find what you need locally, you can contact one of the following sources of supply.

Sources of Supply:

The following companies have an extensive selection of useful products and a long track-record of fulfillment. They have natural body care, aromatherapy, flower essences, crystals and tumbled stones, homeopathy, herbal products, vitamins and supplements, videos, books, audio tapes, candles, incense and bulk herbs, teas, massage tools and products and numerous alternative health items across a wide range of categories.

WHOLESALE:

Wholesale suppliers sell to stores and practitioners, not to individual consumers buying for their own personal use. Individual consumers should contact the RETAIL supplier listed below. Wholesale accounts should contact with business name, resale number or practitioner license in order to obtain a wholesale catalog and set up an account.

Lotus Light Enterprises, Inc.

P. O. Box 1008
Silver Lake, WI 531 70 USA
262 889 8501 (phone)
262 889 8591 (fax)
800 548 3824 (toll free order line)

RETAIL:

Retail suppliers provide products by mail order direct to consumers for their personal use. Stores or practitioners should contact the wholesale supplier listed above.

Internatural

33719 116th Street
Twin Lakes, WI 53181 USA
800 643 4221 (toll free order line)
262 889 8581 office phone
WEB SITE: www.internatural.com

Web site includes an extensive annotated catalog of more than 7000 products that can be ordered "on line" for your convenience 24 hours a day, 7 days a week.